EASY AS VEGAN PIE

One-of-a-Kind Sweet and Savory Slices

By Hannah Kaminsky

Skyhorse Publishing

Skyhorse Publishing books may be purchased in bulk at special discounts for sales promotion, corporate gifts, fund-raising, or educational purposes. Special editions can also be created to specifications. For details, contact the Special Sales Department, Skyhorse Publishing, 307 West 36th Street, 11th Floor, New York, NY 10018 or info@skyhorsepublishing.com.

Skyhorse® and Skyhorse Publishing® are registered trademarks of Skyhorse Publishing, Inc.®, a Delaware corporation.

Visit our website at www.skyhorsepublishing.com.

10 9 8 7 6 5 4 3 2 1

Library of Congress Cataloging-in-Publication Data is available on file.
ISBN: 978-1-62636-102-7
Printed in China

This book wouldn't have been possible without my mom, who cheered me on, fearlessly tasted new recipes, and cleaned up my messes all along the way. P.S., I'm sorry I let you eat the pie that fell in the ocean.

The henna featured on my Mango Chutney Pie is the masterpiece of Cori Burke of Indrani's Mehndi, www.hennaIndrani.com.

Indispensible recipe testers Kelly Cavalier, Melissa Chapman, Carrie Mendolia, Vanessa Pastore, MeShell Gudz, and Cat DiStasio paved the way for smooth sailing through these recipes, preventing future baking disasters.

CONTENTS

INTRODUCTION

W*hy pie?* That very question rattled through my head, day after day . . .

It would be foolish and quite arrogant to claim that an exhaustive, be-all, end-all tome on the subject could come from my hands. Few baked goods carry as much history, or such emotional weight, as pie, with recipes passed down through generations of mothers, sisters, fathers, and brothers. No one will make a pie quite as good as one prepared by a loved one. I don't think that one single book could ever cover all aspects of pies, from their myriad forms and shapes, to the most creative fillings, to that elusive secret formula for "the best crust." No, no such book can honestly exist, so the tome you hold in your hands isn't it . . . But it's *my* take on the noble pie. I may not have learned to roll out pie dough at my grandmother's knee, or honed my skills through years of practice, but it's never too late to pick up a few new tricks.

Pie should never be intimidating or seem out of reach, even to the most inexperienced of bakers. That's why I'd argue that if I, someone so far outside the pie-making fold, can roll with the best of them, anyone else can, too. It's time to end the stereotype that merely making crust can bring newcomers to their knees, placing pies on an unattainable pedestal that scares away those who simply hunger for a slice of comfort. Bring pie back to the table where it belongs, accessible to anyone with the desire to throw down a bit of flour and watch it transform by way of some ancient alchemy into something delicious in the oven.

Take the following instructions with a pinch of salt, and sugar if your sweet tooth does so implore, because no recipe should be set in stone. Experiment fearlessly, fail brilliantly, and succeed with as flamboyant a victory dance as you like. Pie is a dish meant for sharing, so make sure that above all else, you have plenty of company to share your work. Nothing will win new friends like a generous slice of freshly baked pie.

INGREDIENTS GLOSSARY

Agave Nectar

Derived from the same plant as tequila but far less potent, this nectar is the sweet syrup at the core of the agave cactus. It is available in both light and dark varieties; the dark possesses a more nuanced, complex, and somewhat floral flavor, while the light tends to provide only a clean sweetness. Unrefined, agave nectar has a much lower glycemic index than many traditional granulated sweeteners, and is therefore consumed by some diabetics in moderation. Any health food or natural food store worth its stuff should stock agave nectar.

Agar (Agar-Agar)

Known also as kanten, agar is a gelatinous substance made out of seaweed. It is a perfect substitute for traditional gelatin, which is extracted from the collagen within animals' connective tissues and obviously extremely not vegan. Agar comes in both powdered and flaked form. I prefer to use the powder because it is easier to incorporate smoothly into puddings, faster to thicken, and measures gram for gram like standard gelatin. However, if you can only find the flakes, just whiz them in a spice grinder for a few minutes and—voila, instant agar powder! Agar can be found in Asian markets and some health food stores.

All-Purpose Flour

While wonderful flours can be made from all sorts of grains, beans, nuts, and seeds, the gold standard in everyday baking would be "all purpose" wheat flour. Falling texturally somewhere in between cake flour and bread flour, all-purpose flour has the ability to create light desserts which still have substance. It is therefore used most often in my recipes, and stocked as one of my pantry staples. All-purpose flour may be labeled in stores as unbleached white flour or simply "plain flour."

Almond Meal /Flour

Almond flour is the end result of grinding down raw almonds into a fine powder; almond meal is generally a bit coarser. To make your own, just throw a pound or so of completely unadulterated almonds into your food processor, and let the machine work its magic. Due to their high oil content, ground nuts can go rancid fairly quickly. If you opt to stock up and save some for later, be sure to store the freshly ground almond flour in an airtight container in the refrigerator or freezer. To cut down on labor and save a little time, almond flour or meal can be purchased in bulk from natural food stores.

Alum

A throwback to the olden days of food preservation, alum is mainly used for pickling fruits and vegetables, to keep foods crisp in texture and fresh in taste. Still available right next to the allspice in all major grocery stores, it's a potent salt (like sodium or potassium) which must always be used sparingly, as it can prove toxic if ingested in large doses (over 1 ounce at a time.) If the sound of that makes you nervous, feel free to omit the alum when called for. It carries a certain astringent, acidic taste that's hard to describe, but you won't miss it too much if you've never used it in the first place.

Apple Cider Vinegar

As with oil, vinegar can be made from all sorts of fruits, grains, and roots, which all create unique flavor profiles and chemical compositions in the finished product. Thinking along these lines, apple cider vinegar could be considered the olive oil of vinegars; flavorful, useful, and an all-around great thing to have on hand. Regular white wine vinegar or the other standard options would certainly work, but the distinctive "twang" of apple cider vinegar rounds out baked goods so perfectly, and it is so easy to find . . . why wouldn't you use it? Hunt around the oil and salad dressing aisles in your local supermarket, where you should have no problem securing a bottle.

Arrowroot Powder/Flour

Thanks to arrowroot, you can thicken sauces, puddings, and mousses with ease. This white powder is very similar to kudzu and is often compared to other starchy flours. However, arrowroot is so fine that it produces much smoother, creamier results, and is less likely to stick together and form large, glutinous lumps. It freezes very nicely, which is why it's one of my favorite thickeners when making ice cream. Most mega-marts have one or two brands to choose from tucked in among the flours in the baking aisle.

Barley Malt Syrup

A dark brown, thick syrup bearing the distinctive aroma of toasted cereal, barley malt syrup is about half as sweet as sugar, but at least ten times as flavorful. Dark and wholesome, it's an excellent alternative to molasses. Being so sticky, it's a bit trickier to use than the ubiquitous malted milk powder, but contributes a much fuller flavor. Many standard grocery stores now carry it in the natural ingredient section, and no health food store worth its salt would be caught without at least a jar or two on hand.

Black Cocoa Powder

What do you get when you oxidize Dutch-processed cocoa powder to the extreme? Black cocoa, of course! Dark as coal, it certainly lives up to its name and produces amazing jet-black color in baked goods. However, it has a much lower fat content than standard cocoa, and should therefore be used sparingly to avoid altering the texture of your baked goods. I rarely use black cocoa, because it is difficult to find and more expensive than the alternative. Nonetheless, if you wish to create breath-taking chocolate desserts, black cocoa will never fail to impress. You can hunt it down at some tea or spice specialty shops, but if all else fails, a search online should prove fruitful. Feel free to substitute regular Dutch-processed cocoa for an equally tasty, if comparatively pale, dessert.

Black Salt (Kala Namak)

Lovingly if crudely nicknamed "fart salt" around these parts, the sulfurous odor released by a big bagful really does smell like . . . Well, you can probably guess. Despite that unpromising introduction, it does taste far better, and eerily similar to eggs. Enhancing everything from tofu scramble to challah, it's one of those secret ingredients that every vegan should have in their arsenal. Don't let the name confuse you though; the fine grains are actually a mottled pink in appearance, not black.

Brown Rice Syrup

Caramel-colored and thick like honey, brown rice syrup is a natural sweetener that is produced from brown rice. It is less sweet than granulated sugar, adding a wholesome complexity to baked goods. The deep flavor of brown rice syrup is best cast in supporting roles, complementing other aspects of the dish without taking center stage. Brown rice syrup can be found in health food stores across the map, but corn syrup will make a suitable substitute if you are unable to find it locally.

Cacao Nibs

Also known as raw chocolate, cacao nibs are unprocessed cacao nuts, simply broken up into smaller pieces. Much more bitter and harsh than the sweet, mellow chocolate found in bars or chips, it is often used for texture and accent flavor in desserts. Sometimes it can be found coated in sugar to soften its inherent acidity, but for baking, you want the plain, raw version if possible. Seek out bags of cacao nibs in health food stores; if you're really lucky, you may be able to find them in the bulk bins of well-stocked specialty stores.

Chia Seeds

Yes, this is the same stuff that makes chia pets so green and fuzzy, and yes, the seeds are edible! Tiny but mighty, what makes these particular seeds so special is that they form a gel when mixed with liquid. This makes them a powerful binder when trying to replace eggs, or should flaxseeds be in short supply. Store in the freezer for a longer lifespan, and grind them before using in baked goods to maintain an even crumb texture.

Chocolate (Semi-Sweet and Bittersweet)

Chocolate is chocolate, right? One would assume so, but one would be sadly wrong. Obviously milk chocolate is out of the picture, yet some dark and semi-sweet chocolates still don't make the vegan cut. Even those that claim to be "70 percent cacao solids, extra-special dark" may have milk solids or butterfat lurking within. Don't buy the hype or the filler! Stay vigilant and check labels for milk-based ingredients, as unadulterated chocolate is far superior. Semi-sweet has approximately half as much sugar as cocoa solids, and bittersweet tends to have even less.

Chocolate Crème-Filled Sandwich Cookies

As America's favorite cookie, it is no surprise that the Oreo® would come up sooner or later on this list. While the original Oreo® is now changing its ways to take out the trans-fats and animal products, there are many other options that are even more ethically acceptable. Newman's Own makes an excellent organic version that tastes just like the cookies you might remember from your childhood. Plus, along with some exciting flavor variations, Newman-O's (as they are called) can even be found in a wheat-free format! Any Oreo-like cocoa wafers with a vegan crème filling will do, so it is up to your own discretion as to which brand you use.

Cocoa Butter

Chocolate is comprised of two key elements: The cocoa solids, which give it that distinct cocoa flavor, and the cocoa butter, which is the fat that provides the body. Cocoa butter is solid at room temperature, like all tropical oils, so it's best to measure it after melting, as the firm chunks can appear deceptively voluminous. It's really important to pick up high quality, food grade cocoa butter. As a popular ingredient in body lotions and lip balms, some offerings come with fillers and undesirable additives, so shop carefully if you search locally. Also avoid deodorized cocoa butter, unless you'd rather omit its natural flavor from your desserts.

Coconut Flour

It's no wonder this fine powder is so high in fiber—It's essentially dried coconut shreds ground down to a floury consistency. A great option for gluten-free adherents, it has yet to catch on with mainstream bakers so you may need to scope out the local health food store or Whole Foods Market to hunt it down.

Coconut Milk

When called for in this book, I'm referring to regular, full-fat coconut milk. That fat is necessary for a smooth, creamy mouth feel, and of course a richer taste. In the case of ice cream, light coconut milk cannot be substituted without detrimental effects to the final texture. Plain coconut milk is found canned in the ethnic foods aisle of the grocery store. You can make it yourself from fresh coconut meat, but in most cases, such as baking and general dessert-making when it's not the featured flavor, the added hassle honestly isn't worth the expense or effort.

Coconut Oil

Once demonized as artery-clogging sludge not fit to grease a doorframe, nutritionists now can't recommend this tropical fat highly enough. Touted for its benefits when consumed or used on the skin or hair, it's readily available just about anywhere you turn. Two varieties populate store shelves: Virgin (or raw/unrefined) coconut oil and refined coconut oil. Virgin gets the best press from the health experts since it's less processed, and it bears the subtle aroma of the coconut flesh. Refined is wonderful for baked goods, however, since it has been deodorized and is essentially flavorless, allowing it to blend seamlessly with any other flavors. They both solidify below 76 degrees, but virgin oil reaches its smoke point at

350 degrees while refined is at 450 degrees. Either works fine for raw or unbaked treats, but I would recommend refined for baked applications.

Confectioner's Sugar

Otherwise known as powdered sugar, icing sugar, or 10x sugar, confectioner's sugar is a very finely ground version of standard white sugar, often with a touch of starch included to prevent clumping. There are many vegan options on the market, so just keep your eyes open and you will likely find a good supply. You can make your own confectioner's sugar by powdering 1 cup of granulated sugar with 1 tablespoon of cornstarch in your food processor or spice grinder. Simply blend the sugar and cornstarch on the highest speed for about two minutes, allowing the dust to settle before opening your machine—unless you want to inhale a cloud of sugar!

Cream Cheese

Many innovative companies now make dairy-free products that will give you the most authentic cream cheese frostings imaginable. These "cheeses" also hold up beautifully in cookie dough and piecrusts, contributing a great tangy flavor and excellent structure. My favorite brand is the classic Tofutti®, but there are now numerous options available that all work just as well in dessert applications. This ingredient is hard to replace with homemade varieties when seeking smooth, consistent results, so I suggest that you check out your local mega mart or natural food grocer, or head online if all else fails.

Cream of Tartar

Don't let the name fool you; cream of tartar has absolutely nothing to do with either cream or tartar sauce. It is actually created through the fermentation process that grapes undergo in the production of wine. Thus, it can contribute a good deal of acid to recipes in a compact, powdered package. Sometimes used as a stabilizer, it can create flavors similar to buttermilk, or be used to create baking powder: For a small batch, sift together 2 tablespoons cream of tartar with 1 tablespoon baking soda and 1 teaspoon cornstarch.

Creamer

Beware: Vegan creamer is not the same thing as non-dairy creamer! Tricky wordsmiths in the food industry have managed to label their coffee whiteners as "non-dairy" despite the fact that they are actually derived from lactose. Read labels carefully. Vegan creamer based on soy or coconut is a thicker liquid than regular non-dairy milk. While it adds richness and moisture to cakes and creamy spreads, vegan creamers lack the proper ratio of proteins necessary to make whipped cream. Rather, they consist primarily of sugars, and consequently boast a sweeter taste. Soy and coconut creamers are available in a number of flavors, all of which may be used for some additional flavoring, if desired. In a pinch, regular soymilk or other milk alternatives can be substituted, although the end results might not be quite as rich.

EnerG Egg Replacer®

Although I'm typically resistant to calling for brand name mixes such as the powdered egg replacer indicated here, it simply isn't possible to make some of the more delicate (and traditionally egg-white based) cookies and pastries with anything else. If you want your vegan meringues and macarons, you'll just have to bite the bullet and buy a box. It's a small price to pay for creating the "impossible" vegan meringue, if you ask me. EnerG is available online and in most health food stores.

Five-Spice Powder

A powerful mixture of anise, pepper, cinnamon, fennel seed, and cloves, we owe Chinese cuisine for this spicy representation of the five basic tastes—Salty, sweet, sour, bitter, and savory. Ratios and exact blends vary depending on who you ask, and every cook seems to have their own family recipe, so go ahead and tweak until it pleases your own palate. Most grocery stores will stock the seasoning in the spice aisle, but here's how I like to mix mine up at home:

2 Tablespoons Ground Star Anise

2 Tablespoons Crushed Cinnamon Stick Pieces

2 Teaspoons Ground Fennel Seeds

2 Teaspoons Crushed Szechuan Peppercorns

¼ Teaspoon Ground Cloves

Toss all of the spices into a coffee or spice grinder, and just let the machine pulverize everything to a fine powder. Make sure that there are no large pieces or unmixed pockets of spice before transferring to an airtight jar. Dark-colored glass is the best option, because light will degrade the flavors faster.

If you can't find Szechuan peppercorns, an equal amount of either black or white peppercorns can be substituted for a slightly different but similarly fiery bite.

Flavor Extracts

I usually try to stay as far away from extracts as possible, because they are all too often artificial, insipid, and a poor replacement for the real thing. However, real vanilla and almond are my two main exceptions, as high quality extracts from the actual sources are readily available in most markets. Just make sure to avoid any bottles that contain sugar, corn syrup, colors, or chemical stabilizers in addition to your flavor of choice. For some of the more unusual extracts, if your supermarket searches end up unsuccessful, try the Internet.

Flaxseeds

Ground flaxseeds make an excellent vegan egg-replacer when combined with water. One tablespoon of the whole seeds produces approximately 1½ tablespoons of the ground powder. While you can purchase pre-ground flax seed meal in many stores, I prefer to grind the flax seeds fresh for each recipe, as they tend to go rancid rather quickly once broken down. Not to mention, it takes mere seconds to powder your own flax seeds in a spice grinder! If you do opt to purchase flax meal instead, be sure to store the powder in your refrigerator or freezer until you are ready to use it. These tiny seeds can be found in bulk bins and prepackaged in the baking aisle of natural food stores.

Garbanzo (Chickpea) Flour

Gaining in popularity as a versatile gluten-free flour, garbanzo flour is just what you might imagine; nothing but dried, ground chickpeas! Although it is now used primarily in baking, to substitute for wheat flours and to add a certain density to cakes or cookies, it can also be cooked with water like polenta, and eaten either as a hot porridge or let set overnight in a baking dish, sliced, and then fried to make what is called chickpea panisse. Just be warned that eaten raw (if, say, someone decided to sample raw cookie batter that contains garbanzo flour) it is very bitter and unpleasant.

Garbanzo flour should be readily available in most grocery stores in the baking or natural foods section, but if you have a powerful blender like a Vita-Mix® (see Kitchen Toys and Tools) with a dry grinding container, you can make your own from dried, split chickpeas (also known as chana dal. Process 2 cups of legumes at a time, and use the plunger to keep things moving. Once finely ground, let the dust settle for a few minutes before removing the lid of the container.

Graham Crackers and Graham Cracker Crumbs

When I first went searching for vegan graham crackers, I was appalled at my lack of options. Why every brand in sight needed to include honey was beyond me. So, what is a hungry vegan baker to do in a tight situation like this? Keep on looking, of course. Concealed among the rest, and often in natural foods stores, there are a few brands that exclude all animal products. You can of course make your own, following the recipe on page 42. Once you secure your crackers, you have two options to turn them into crumbs. For a coarse, more varied crumb, toss them into a sturdy plastic bag and just go at it with a rubber mallet or rolling pin. To achieve a fine, even crumb, grind them down in your food processor or spice grinder.

Graham Flour

Most commonly found in crackers, graham flour is simply a fancy type of wheat flour. It is made from a process that separates all parts of the wheat kernel itself, and recombines them in different proportions. For reasons beyond my grasp, this particular flour is not sold in all countries. If you are having a hard time getting your hands on some, and don't mind an end product with a slightly different texture, regular whole wheat flour can be substituted. Of course, you may be able to locate graham flour online and save yourself the worry altogether.

Granulated Sugar

Yes, plain old, regular white sugar. Surprised to see this basic sweetener here? It's true that all sugar (beet or cane) is derived from plant sources and therefore vegan by nature. However, there are some sneaky things going on behind the scenes in big corporations these days. Some cane sugar is filtered using bone char, a very non-vegan process, but that will never be specified on a label. If you're not sure about the brand that you typically buy, your best bet is to contact the manufacturer directly and ask.

To bypass this problem, many vegans purchase unbleached cane sugar. While it is a suitable substitute, unbleached cane sugar does have a higher molasses content than white sugar, so it has more of a brown sugar-like flavor, and tends to produce desserts that are denser. Luckily, there are a few caring companies that go to great pains to ensure the purity of their sugar products, such as Florida Crystals® and Amalgamated Sugar Company®, the suppliers to White Satin, Fred Meyer, Western Family, and Parade. I typically opt for one of these vegan sugar brands to get the best results. You can often find appropriate sugar in health food store bulk bins these days to save some money, but as always, verify the source before forking over the cash. As sugar can be a touchy vegan subject, it is best to use your own judgment when considering which brand to purchase.

Green Pea Flour

Just like garbanzo (or any other bean) flour, green pea flour is the dried and ground powder of its namesake. It's a bit more unusual than most due to its startling color, and it's harder to come by in local markets. Bob's Red Mill produces it in 24-ounce bags, which are readily available on Amazon.com.

Instant Coffee Powder

Though completely unfit for drinking as intended, instant coffee powder is an ideal way to add those crave-worthy roasted, smoky notes to any dessert without also incorporating a lot of extra liquid. Stored in the fridge, a small jar should last a long time. You can even find decaf versions, in case you're more sensitive to caffeine but still want that flavor in your recipes. I prefer powder to granules because it dissolves more easily, but both can work interchangeably with a bit of vigorous mixing.

Maple Syrup

One of my absolute favorite sweeteners, there is simply no substitute for real, 100 percent maple syrup. The flavor is like nothing else out there, and I have yet to meet a single brand of pancake syrup that could even come close. Of course, this incredible indulgence does come at a hefty price. Though it would be absolute sacrilege to use anything but authentic grade B maple syrup on pancakes or waffles in my house, I will sometimes bend the rules in recipes where it isn't such a prominent flavor, in order to save some money. In these instances, I'll substitute with a maple-agave blend, which still carries the flavor from the actual source, but bulks it up with an equal dose of agave for sweetening power. Grade A is a fine substitute in a pinch, but contrary to what the letter would suggest, it's actually less flavorful than Grade B.

Maraschino Cherries

Lurid red marbles that bear only a passing resemblance to the fresh fruits they once were, maraschino cherries are generally an ingredient I avoid at all costs. However, for the sake of nostalgia and preserving the integrity of certain classic flavor combinations, I have been known to make a few exceptions. What I take issue with most is the intense (and vaguely bitter) artificial coloring and syrupy sweetness, typically contributed by high-fructose corn syrup. Thankfully, with a bit of hunting, you can find natural alternatives out there. Versions produced by Luxardo®, Silver Palate®, and Tillen Farms®, for example, contain no preservatives and are colored solely by fruit and vegetable extracts. They can be found in specialty grocery stores and online.

Matcha/Maccha Powder

Perhaps one of my all-time favorite flavorings, matcha is a very high-quality powdered green tea. It is used primarily in Japanese tea ceremonies and can have an intense, complex, and bitter taste when used in large amounts. Contrary to what many new bakers think, this is NOT the same as the green tea leaves you'll find in mega mart tea bags! Those are vastly inferior in the flavor department, and real matcha is ground much finer. There are many levels of quality, with each step up in grade carrying a higher price tag. Because it can become quite pricey, I would suggest buying a medium grade, which should be readily available at any specialty tea store. When translated directly from Japanese, the spelling is "maccha," but the typical English spelling is matcha. Whichever way the package is labeled, you will still find green tea powder within.

Millet Flour

Wheat-free and appropriate for those on gluten-free diets when sourced carefully, millet flour has a subtly nutty flavor and fine texture. It has absolutely no binding powers by itself, and must be combined with a blend of other flours to make a cohesive baked good. Though it's one of the less common flours out there, most health food stores will have at least one or two brands of bagged millet flour.

Mochiko

Mochiko is simply finely ground mochi flour, or glutinous rice flour. You can find this in any Asian specialty market or online. Koda Farms® is one of the most common brands available in the US; it can be purchased in compact, white 1-pound boxes.

Non-Dairy Margarine

It is a basic kitchen staple, but good margarine can actually be quite elusive if you do not know what to look for. Some name brands contain whey or other milk-derivatives, while others conceal the elusive, animal-derived Vitamin D3, so be alert when scanning ingredient labels. For ease, I prefer to use stick margarine, such as Earth Balance® Buttery Sticks. Never try to substitute spreadable margarine from a tub! These varieties have much more water to allow them to spread while cold, and will thus bake differently. I always use unsalted margarine unless otherwise noted, but you are welcome to use salted as long as you remove about ¼ teaspoon of salt from the recipe. Overly salted food is one of the first flaws that diners notice, so take care with your seasoning!

Non-Dairy Milk

The foundation of many cream and custard pies, I kept this critical ingredient somewhat ambiguous for a reason. Most types of non-dairy milk will work in these recipes, and I wouldn't want to limit anyone with specific allergies. The only type that I absolutely do not recommend using is rice milk, as it tends to be much thinner, often gritty, and completely lacking in the body necessary to make rich, satisfying desserts. Unless explicitly specified, any other type of vegan milk-substitute will work. My top pick is unsweetened almond milk because it tends to be a bit thicker, richer, and still has a neutral flavor. Don't be afraid to experiment, though; there's a lot to choose from!

Nutritional Yeast

Unlike active yeast, nutritional yeast is not used to leaven baked goods, but to flavor all sorts of dishes. Prized for its distinctly savory, cheesy flavor, it's a staple in most vegan pantries and is finally starting to gain recognition in mainstream cooking as well. Though almost always found in savory recipes, I sometimes like to add a tiny pinch to particular desserts, bringing out its more subtle buttery characteristics. There is no substitute for nutritional yeast, so if you can't find it, your best bet here is to simply leave it out.

Orange Blossom Water

Distilled from bitter-orange flowers, this delicately perfumed extract isn't citrus flavored, but floral. A little bit goes a long way, so even a small bottle should last you a good, long time. Middle Eastern markets are your best bet for reasonably priced options. In a pinch, rose water can work instead.

Panko Bread Crumbs

This Japanese import is much crisper and more airy than so-called "Italian-style" bread crumbs. That unique texture allows it to better resist absorbing oil when fried, yielding lighter, less greasy coatings. When used as filler or binder within recipes, it has a less prominent wheat flavor, allowing it to blend seamlessly into the background of just about anything, sweet or savory.

Phyllo Dough

Alternately spelled "fillo" or "filo" dough, this gossamer-thin pastry is not something for the average cook (or even most highly skilled ones) to attempt at home. Rather, it's much more sensible to buy it frozen at the grocery store, where most brands should be vegan. Just double-check labels for any sneaky dairy derivatives that may be lurking, and all the rest should be good.

Red Wine

While I don't actually drink, I can tell you that if your wine isn't something you'd want in a glass, it's not something you'd want in a cake or sorbet, either. Avoid so-called "cooking wines" and just go with something moderately priced, and on the sweeter side to compliment the dessert that it's going into. Don't be afraid to ask for help when you go shopping; the people who work at wine stores tend to have good advice about these things! Be vigilant and do your homework though, because not all wines are vegan. Shockingly, some are filtered through isinglass, which is actually made from fish bladders! So, to avoid a fishy brew, double check brands on http://www.barnivore.com/wine.

Salt

The importance of salt in desserts cannot be overstated. It's that spark that makes flavors pop and balances out a bit of the sweetness that might otherwise overwhelm the palate. To make a long story short, you do not want to leave out this unassuming but critical ingredient! Unless otherwise noted, I use regular old table salt (finely ground) in baking. Flaky sea salt or kosher salt can be fun to sprinkle directly over finished baked goods before serving for an extra punch of flavor, but be careful not to overdo it; there's a fine line between salted and downright salty.

Sour Cream

Another creative alternative comes to the rescue of vegan bakers everywhere! Vegan sour cream provides an amazingly similar yet dairy-free version of the original tangy spread. In a pinch, I suppose you might be able to get away with using soy yogurt instead, but that is generally much thinner, so I really wouldn't recommend it. Vegan "sour cream" is sold in natural food stores and some mainstream grocers. It can often be found neatly tucked in among its dairy-based rivals, or with the other refrigerated dairy alternatives.

Sprinkles

What's a birthday party without a generous handful of sprinkles to brighten up the cake? Though these colorful toppers are made primarily of edible wax, they are often coated in confectioner's glaze, which is code for mashed up insects, to give them their lustrous shine. Happily, you can now find specifically vegan sprinkles (sold as "sprinkelz") produced by the Let's Do® company, in both chocolate and colored versions, which can be found at just about any natural food store.

Tahini

An irreplaceable staple in Middle Eastern cuisine, most regular grocery stores should be able to accommodate your tahini requests. Tahini is a paste very much like peanut butter, but made from sesame seeds rather than nuts. If you don't have any on hand and a trip to the market is not in your immediate plans, then any other nut butter will provide exactly the same texture within a recipe, though it will impart a different overall taste. You can also make your own, just like you would make nut butter, but a high-speed blender is highly recommended to achieve a smooth texture.

Tofu

Yes, I make desserts with tofu and I'm not ashamed to admit it! When I use tofu for baked goods and ice creams, I always reach for the aseptic, shelf stable packs. Not only do they seem to last forever when unopened, but they also blend down into a perfectly smooth liquid when processed thoroughly, not a trace of grit or off-flavors to be found. The most common brand is Mori-Nu®, which is widely available, especially in Japanese and natural food stores, so just keep an eye peeled and you should have no problem locating it.

Turbinado Sugar

Coarse, light brown granulated sugar, I just love the sparkle that this edible glitter lends when applied to the outside of cookies. Though it's not the best choice for actually baking with since the large crystals make for an uneven distribution of sweetness, it adds a satisfying crunch and eye-appeal when used as decoration. Turbinado sugar is very easy to find in the baking department of any typical grocery store or mega mart.

Vanilla (Extract, Paste, and Beans)

One of the most important ingredients in a baker's arsenal, vanilla is found in countless forms and qualities. It goes without saying that artificial flavorings pale in comparison to the real thing. Madagascar vanilla is the traditional full-bodied vanilla that most people appreciate in desserts, so stick with that and you can't go wrong. Happily, it's also the most common and moderately priced variety. To take your desserts up a step, vanilla paste brings in the same amount of flavor, but includes those lovely little vanilla bean flecks that makes everyone think you busted out the good stuff and used whole beans. Vanilla paste can be substituted 1:1 for vanilla extract. Like whole vanilla beans, save the paste for things where you'll really see those specks of vanilla goodness, like ice creams, custards, and frostings. Vanilla beans, the most costly but flavorful option, can be used instead, at about 1 bean per 2 teaspoons of extract or paste.

Once you've split and scraped out the insides, don't toss that vanilla pod! Get the most for your money by stashing it in a container of granulated sugar, to slowly infuse the sugar with delicious vanilla flavor. Alternately, just store the pod in a container until it dries out, and then grind it up very finely in a high-speed blender and use it to augment a good vanilla extract. The flavor won't be nearly as strong as the seeds, but it does contribute to the illusion that you've used the good stuff.

Wafer Cookie Crumbs

Made from flat, crunchy cookies that are available in a wide variety of shapes and flavors, there are quite a few vegan options on the market. Just be sure to check the ingredient and allergen statement, and stay away from those that look soft or chewy. For a thrifty endeavor, you could also try baking your own at home! See page 48 for recipes. With your cookies at the ready, pulverize them into crumbs using a food processor, spice grinder, or a good old-fashioned rubber mallet, depending upon your mood. I prefer to crush mine fairly finely, so that it resembles something like almond meal, but a rough crumble can lend a rustic charm, too.

Wasabi Paste and Powder

Just like the mounds of green paste served with sushi, the prepared wasabi paste found in tubes is almost certainly not made of wasabi root. Strange but true, it's typically colored horseradish instead, due to the rarity and expense of real wasabi. Read labels carefully, because it's one of those things that seems guaranteed to be vegan-friendly, but can give you a nasty surprise if you're not careful. Milk derivatives are often added, for reasons I couldn't begin to explain. Wasabi powder can be potent stuff indeed, but only if it's extremely fresh. The flavor dissipates over time, so be sure to toss any that has been sitting in your pantry well past its prime. If quality paste is nowhere to be found, opt for prepared horseradish (blended only with a dash of vinegar) instead. In some cases, mustard powder can lend a similar flavor instead of wasabi powder, but only in very small doses.

Whipped Cream

Still something of a novelty, ready-to-use aerosol cans of vegan whipped "cream" do exist in Whole Foods Markets and many specialty health food stores. Made by Soyatoo®, it can be found in both rice- and soy-based versions, and sprays out fluffy and lightly sweetened every time. MimicCream® also makes a whippable nut-based cream called "Healthy Top," sold in aseptic packages, which is to be beaten like traditional cream. Unfortunately, these toppings are very expensive, so it's much more practical, and nearly as easy, to make your own whipped topping from scratch (page 52).

White Whole Wheat Flour

Move over whole wheat pastry flour, healthy bakers everywhere have a new best friend! It may look and taste like regular white flour, but it's actually milled from the whole grain. Simply made from hard white wheat berries instead of red, the color and flavor is much lighter, making it the perfect addition to nearly every sort of baking application you can think of. If you're concerned about getting more fiber into your diet, feel free to switch out the all-purpose flour in any recipe in this book for white whole wheat.

Yogurt

Fermented by good bacteria that are said to improve your digestion, yogurt now comes in just about any flavor, color, or non-dairy formulation you can imagine. Soy yogurts or "soygurts" are found at pretty much any grocery store these days, and you can even find some that are agave-sweetened, too. For those with soy allergies, don't despair, there are also delicious coconut and almond yogurts available. Just double-check that whatever you decide to buy is certified as vegan; just because it's non-dairy doesn't mean it uses vegan cultures. Greek-style yogurts are thicker than the traditional options, much more like sour cream in consistency, and are currently only produced by So Delicious®, in both almond and coconut varieties. The big, multi-serving tubs are handy if you plan to do a lot of baking, but I generally prefer to purchase single-serving, 6-ounce containers for baking, to avoid leftovers that may go bad while waiting for a new application to come along. Please note, however, that one container of yogurt does not equal one cup; 6 ounces will be equivalent to about ¾ cup by volume measure. It does help to have a food scale if you decide to buy in bulk, though, so that you can weigh out the amount that would be found in one standard container.

Easy as Vegan Pie

KITCHEN TOOLS AND TOYS

As centuries of bakers have proven, you don't need any fancy equipment to turn out pies so good you'll want to devour the whole thing without sharing a single slice. At bare minimum, you'll need a few large bowls, a spatula, a pie tin, a working oven, and plenty of elbow grease. All the rest is non-obligatory, but does make the work move along much more easily. There's no shame in getting a helping hand from modern technology when possible. Here are a few options that may aid in your pie adventures:

Blender

They come in all shapes and sizes, with wildly varying prices to match. If you want the sturdiest machine that will grant you the most pureeing power, I can't recommend the Vita-Mix® highly enough. Yes, it's one of the priciest models on the market for consumer purchase, but it actually is professional quality and will pay for itself through saved time and aggravation. There is simply nothing else that can blend whole nuts so silky smooth, or grind whole beans down to perfectly fine flour. I use mine almost every day, whether for baking adventures or just blending myself a smoothie.

Cookie Cutters

When we're talking about pie motifs, both functional and decorative, I reach for small to medium-sized plastic cutters whenever possible, which are free of intricate details. Shapes that are too complex tend to stretch and distort when the upper crust is applied. Just because you can buy a 1-inch baby fawn cookie cutter doesn't mean cut-outs will look like fawns once baked! Plastic is my favorite material because it doesn't bend or rust over time.

Food Processor

They both have a spinning blade at the bottom of a sealed canister, but don't consider a blender and a food processor as being interchangeable in every procedure. There's no way you'd be able to make pastry dough in a blender, but my food processor is the secret to effortlessly whipping up one flaky crust after another. If you only have space in your budget for one, go for the food processor, especially if you're particularly fond of pies. Opt for a model with at least 7–8 cups capacity, or else be prepared to process many recipes in batches.

Ice Cream Maker

One of the top kitchen toys on many foodies' wish lists, ice cream makers are no longer the frivolous luxuries reserved only for those with a bit too much money and time on their hands. All you need is a basic model that can churn at least 1–2 quarts of ice cream at a time. The most reasonably priced options are those that have detachable bowls that you freeze solid before using, and start at about $50 brand new. Self-freezing units allow you to churn up much more ice cream in a fraction of the time, but start around the $150 mark and can skyrocket up to about $1000, so for the casual ice cream enthusiast, simpler is by far better. High or low end, Cuisinart® is the gold standard for my ice cream churning needs.

Kitchen Torch

Hasn't every child wanted their own flamethrower growing up? Okay, maybe I was just an odd child, but there's no denying the allure of playing with fire. A kitchen torch allows you that thrill with a bit more safety than the average conflagration. Found in kitchen supply and specialty shops, these devices look somewhat like small guns and are powered by butane. Very reasonably priced at $10–$20 for most basic models, they make brûléeing or browning meringue a breeze. They may look like toys, but you still shouldn't let the kids get their hands on them.

Pastry Brush

Go ahead, take the low-tech route for this one; a good-quality paintbrush that's never been used on anything but food is perfectly fine here. Cheaper brushes will shed and leave bristles behind, so at least spring for a reputable brand. Be careful to seek out those with nylon bristles rather than the traditional horse hair. Actual pastry brushes are now frequently made with different configurations of silicon "bristles," which all work to varying degrees. I'm not a big fan of these, since glazes never seem to stick long enough to make it to the targeted food surface, but they're at least easier to wash since they're dishwasher-safe.

Pastry Cutter/Blender

Think of a horseshoe-shaped tool with a handle on top that holds parallel sets of four to five dull blades at the bottom. The conventional pastry cutter certainly has its place, and for those without a food processor to speed the creation of pastry dough, this handheld tool is the way to go. Always opt for stainless steel with a smooth, comfortable handle. Thinner metal blades are likely to bend over time, so double-check for durability before purchasing. If you're in a jam and need pie ASAP, two forks with long tines can make an adequate substitute.

Pie Birds

Though adorable and charming with their old-school style, pie birds are one of the most useless "tools" you could keep in your kitchen, to put it bluntly. Rarely do these antiquated figurines show up in a modern baker's arsenal, but they were at the height of their popularity around the 1940s. Designed as a clever pun on the classic nursery rhyme, "Four and twenty blackbirds, baked in a pie . . . ," any simple tube or funnel shape could have worked as well, since they're intended to act as miniature chimneys, allowing steam inside a double-crusted pie to escape. Of course, a few simple slits will vent any pastry just fine, and thus the pie bird has very little utility in the real world. Don't bother seeking one out, and if you already have one, donate it to your local thrift store to clear up space for a real kitchen instrument.

Pie Pans

An obvious necessity, but one all too often taken for granted. Size and capacity are the most critical considerations, but the material it's made of will affect your pie as well. Ceramic models have the most charm, adorned with all sorts of colors and designs on the outside, which make them perfect for an oven-to-table presentation. Just like glass pans, they bake evenly and retain heat well, which are good qualities for producing uniformly browned, crisp crusts. Metal pans are always the most inexpensive choice, and what they lack in charm, they make up for in durability. They're ideal for any chilled or frozen dough that needs to go straight into a hot oven, as that kind of stress could easily shatter the aforementioned options. Metal heats especially quickly, so it's best suited for pies that have shorter baking times. Disposable aluminum tins are the final option to consider: Perfect for gifts or potlucks, they're fine as expendable vessels, but have no place in the oven. Bake your pie in a sturdier pan of equal size, let it cool completely (and chill, depending on the recipe) before loosening the edges and sliding the whole thing into the tin. For particularly hefty pies, reinforce the bottom by stacking a second disposable tin underneath.

Pie Shields

Since many pies must be baked for longer than your average pastry, overly browned edges are a frequent concern. A simple tent of aluminum foil usually does the trick, but if you only want to protect the rim of a single crust, that's where a pie shield comes in handy. They're either solid aluminum rings or adjustable silicon strips that go right over the edge of the pie. While helpful on occasion, I've never had particularly good luck with them, crushing the carefully crimped pastry design more often than preserving it. For those rare moments when it would be convenient, I'd recommend the silicon type, since it can accommodate larger or smaller pans more easily.

Pie Weights

A controversial subject in the pie world, pie weights come in all shapes, sizes, and densities. Some claim that the only choice is ceramic marbles on chains, thanks to their ability to distribute heat evenly, and the ease of collecting them after the baking is done. Trust me, removing 375-degree marbles from a still-soft crust is not a fun venture to attempt! They're infinitely reusable, so if you plan on making many pies in your lifetime, two 1-pound sets would be a wise investment. Personally, I tend to go with what I have on hand, which is a big handful of either dried beans or rice. Though more difficult to remove when the baking is done, they're cheap, plentiful, and easy to find. You won't want to eat your grains or beans after they've seen the heat of the oven, but you can reuse them at least a half dozen times, or until they begin to crumble.

Piping/Pastry Bags and Tips

The very first time I picked up a piping bag to frost a cupcake, I knew that there was no going back. It just makes for a more professional presentation than frosting blobbed on with a knife. Piping bags are by no means necessary tools, but rather a baker's luxury. If you don't know how to wield a pastry bag or cannot be bothered with the hassle, there is no need to run out and buy one. However, should you wish to give piping a try, don't skimp on the quality! Piping bags come in heavy-duty, reusable fabric or plastic and disposable varieties, which range in quality. This is one time when I like to use disposable, because piping bags really are a nightmare to clean. Just avoid the cheaper plastic bags, as they are often too thin to stand up to the pressure. As for the tips, you only need one or two big star tips to make a nice "swirly" design. You can also pipe straight out of the bag for a rounded spiral.

Rolling Pins

It's pretty crazy how a tool so simple can come in so many shapes, colors, designs, and prices. Truth be told, you really don't need to buy a rolling pin; a long, smooth-sided bottle can absolutely do the trick, especially if the glass is thick and heavy. Of course, it's much easier to work with a rolling pin that has handles and a longer surface to work with, so it's worth purchasing at least a basic model. Wooden pins are cheap, but lightweight and prone to absorbing flavors and moisture, which makes dough stickier, harder to work with, and potentially less tasty. Better choices include stainless steel and non-stick models, which are easier to clean and have more heft to them for beating down your dough. My top choice goes to marble though, which really stands the test of time. My marble rolling pin is older than I am, and still shows no sign of wear. It's a solid investment (literally) that will last you a lifetime.

Silpats®

I simply adore these flat, nonstick mats and use them at every opportunity. Likened to re-usable parchment paper, silpats cut down on the cost and excess waste of traditional single-use fibers. In terms of performance, silpats also tend to reduce browning, so that it is more difficult (but by no means impossible) to burn cookies when using them. While one should last you several years, it is helpful to have a few on hand. For best care, wash them promptly after each use with mild soap and a soft sponge. Silpats can be located at any decent kitchen store and many grocery stores in the housewares aisle.

Stand Mixer

While hand mixers get the job done, a good stand mixer will save your arm a tremendous amount of grief. A high-quality stand mixer can be a steep initial investment, but it is usually worth its weight in gold. Powerful and independent, it is easy to multitask while this machine mixes away. If your kitchen space or budget doesn't allow for this luxury, then a hand mixer, or even the vigorous use of a whisk, will work whenever a stand mixer is suggested.

Strainer

When I call for one of these in a recipe, chances are I'm not talking about a pasta colander, with its large, spread-out holes. To sieve out raspberry seeds, drain vegan yogurt, or take care of any other liquid/solid separation jobs, a decent fine mesh sieve will tackle the job with ease. Seek out strainers with solid construction, so that the mesh won't pull out after repeated pressings with a spatula. One about 7–9 inches in diameter should accommodate most projects, but bigger is just fine too.

ESSENTIAL TECHNIQUES

Mastering a few simple procedures frequently called for in both baking and cooking will make any culinary task much less daunting. Skills are gained only through experience, so get into the kitchen and start practicing! Even the most timid novices should be able to get these basics down pat in no time.

Rolling Out Pie Dough

Warmth is the mortal enemy of pie dough, so always keep your crusts chilled. That means you should leave them in the fridge until the very last minute, handle them as little as possible, and keep them on the counter only as long as they need to be there. As the dough warms up, the margarine begins to melt, so the dough will become stickier and thus harder to work with, not to mention the fact that you will lose flakiness in the final baked crust. From the moment it hits your lightly floured counter, it should get your full attention. Turn the disk over in the flour to coat both sides, so that it doesn't stick to either the counter or your rolling pin. You can add a pinch of additional flour to the top if it seems to cling at any point.

Start in the center of the disk and apply firm but gentle pressure outwards with your rolling pin, smoothing out the dough as evenly as you can. Roll a few times in one direction, gently lift and turn the dough, and roll again in a new direction. It's easiest if you can stand at a corner, so you can change position more and move the dough around less. Don't worry that it's not a perfect circle (it never will be, even after you've made a million pies). Focus on thickness; even thickness is the key to even baking. An eighth of an inch is the magic measurement that works best to support a filling without burning to a crisp or remaining doughy, so use a ruler or just pretend you're making thin cookies.

Some people prefer to roll out dough between two pieces of parchment paper or silpats to get around the use of flour, thus preventing possible messes. I'm not a big fan of this method since my crusts still stuck to the paper and were more likely to tear upon removal, but this method may be more effective in colder climates.

Transferring Dough to a Pie Pan

So you've got your thin round of dough, ready to use. Now what? It's time to maneuver it into your vessel of choice, a 9-inch round standard pie pan unless otherwise specified in the particular recipe you're making. Since the shape of the crust is rather unwieldy as it stands, I like to make mine more compact for an easy transfer. Very gently fold the whole round in half, without pressing down on the seam or sides, and then fold it in half again in the same fashion, so that it's ultimately a quarter of its former size. Lift the folded round from underneath, handling it lightly, and place the folded point right in the center of your pan. Fully unfold it to fill the dish, easing it up the sides and pressing any creases flat again. You should have more or less even amounts of excess dough overhanging the edges if you've situated it correctly.

Fluting or Crimping the Crust

Neaten up the edges before attempting anything fancy, so that you have the same amount of material to work with all the way around. Use kitchen shears or a very sharp knife to trim the excess dough to about ½ inch away from the rim of the pan. For a single crust, lift up that edge and fold it underneath itself, so that it's resting on the lip of the pie pan and the cut edge is hidden. Continue folding all the way around, straightening and smoothing as you go. The simplest crimp is made with the tines of a fork; just press the fork into the rim again and again until the lines match up in the place where you began. My favorite sort of crimp is done with just three fingers; use two fingers on one hand to press the interior side of the lip, and one finger on the other to press the opposite side of the crust in the center of those two fingers. Repeat all the way around to form a tight scalloped design. For a larger, loopy scallop, turn that single finger into a hook and press that into the side of the crust, using your opposite hands to indent the larger space on either side of the "U" shape.

Making a Double-Crusted Pie

Prepare your bottom crust in the same fashion as you would for a single crust, right up to the stage of trimming away the excess dough from the sides of the pan. Smooth your prepared filling into the bottom crust.

Roll out the second disk of dough on a lightly floured surface to ⅛ inch in thickness. If you wish to make decorative window vents with small cookie cutters, now is the time to punch them out. Fold the dough in half very gently without pressing down, and then fold in half once more so that the round is ultimately quartered. Ease the dough over the top of the filling, centering the folded point to the best of your ability. Carefully unfold the dough, without pulling or stretching, so that it covers the whole surface of the pie. Trim the extra away to about ½-inch overhanging the pan, so that the raw edges of both the top and bottom crusts more or less match up. Run a lightly moistened finger all the way around the outer edges where the two crusts meet; this will act as the "glue" that seals them together. Fold the cut edges underneath themselves, so that they're resting on the lip of the pie pan. Continue folding all the way around, straightening and smoothing as you go. Crimp or decorate as desired. Use a very sharp knife to slice vents out of the top if you haven't cut out shapes with cookie cutters. At least six 1-inch slits radiating evenly around the center should do the trick. Bake according to the recipe's instructions.

Making a Lattice Top

Prepare your bottom crust as you would a plain single crust, up to the step of trimming away the excess dough from the sides of the pan. Smooth your prepared filling into the bottom crust. Roll out the second disk of dough on a lightly floured surface to ⅛ inch in thickness. Cut the round into ¼–½ inch wide strips, depending on how you'd like the lattice to look. Thicker strips will show less of the filling in between, whereas thinner will put a greater area of the filling on display; which you'd like for your creation is purely personal preference.

Place strips across the top of the pie, all going in one direction and spaced about 1 inch apart. Then, turn the pie 90 degrees and place the next strip across the center of the pie so that it's perpendicular to the previous ones. As you lay it across the pie, gently fold back every other strip that it crosses, then lay that one back down over the new strip, effectively weaving it in. Place the next piece about 1 inch away from the first one, and repeat this process with the alternate perpendicular pieces as you come across them. Continue until the top is covered, and don't worry if you have strips leftover. Finally, trim the strip ends so that they match up with the cut edges of the bottom crust. Lightly moisten the edges where they meet the rim of the bottom crust, so that they adhere. Fold the raw edges underneath themselves, so that they're resting on the lip of the pie pan. Continue folding all the way around, straightening and smoothing as you go. Crimp as desired and bake according to the instructions in the recipe.

Making Decorative Crusts and Cut-Outs

If you should find yourself with leftover scraps of dough, don't throw them away—you can use them to make fancy decorations on top of your pie! Just use any small, simple-shaped cookie cutters to punch out your pieces. Adhere them to either the exposed rim of a single crust or the top of a double crust in exactly the same way: Use a lightly moistened finger to dampen the back of your shape before firmly pressing it into place. If you want to decorate the entire border of the pie, this method can take the place of a traditional crimped edge.

Blind-Baking

Baking an empty crust, otherwise known as blind-baking, is necessary for pies with fillings that are not cooked in the oven, or those that would not have the opportunity to cook properly with just one trip through the hot box. This is where many a crust has gone awry, because the filling is what weighs it down and keeps it in place while baking. To prevent your pastry from shrinking or sliding down the sides of the pan, you've got to be a little bit crafty.

Preheat your oven to 425 degrees. Line your pan with pastry as previously instructed and crimp the edges any way your heart desires. Prick the bottom with a fork at approximately 1-inch intervals—this process is known as "docking." Lay a sheet of parchment paper cut to size directly over the interior of the crust, including the sides. Don't be tempted to use foil or anything else in this case; all other materials will stick horrifically, even if greased in advance. Fill the dish with pie weights (see page 19 for pie weight suggestions) and bake for about 15 minutes, until the sides begin to brown.

Retrieve the pie from the oven and carefully remove the weights, as they will still be hot. Gently peel away the parchment since the crust will still be somewhat malleable. If the crust is still pale on the bottom, reduce the oven temperature to 375 and bake for an additional 5–10 minutes, just until golden. Let cool completely before filling.

Bear in mind that this method is only applicable to pastry-based crusts, and not cookie crusts. Graham and cookie crusts are less finicky and can simply be baked empty without any additional fuss, as directed according to the recipe.

Creating the Perfect Golden-Brown Finish

All it takes for any food to cook to a mouth-watering shade of amber is a bit of heat and either sugar or protein. Protein enables the Maillard reaction, whereas sugars create caramelization. Either way, it all leads to one conclusion: Delicious, beautiful food. In the case of pastries, the dough naturally contains a bit of each macronutrient, which allows browning in the oven without further intervention. If you want to enhance that reaction, and potentially add a touch of shine, that's where a swipe of Golden Pastry Glaze comes in handy.

1 Teaspoon Arrowroot
1 Teaspoon Light Corn Syrup
3 Tablespoons Water

Whisk ingredients together vigorously, to dissolve the arrowroot smoothly into the liquid. Use a pastry brush, basting brush, or large art brush that has never been used with paint, to apply the glaze to the upper crust or exposed edges of a single crust. Bake as per usual.

Alternately, plain non-dairy milk can also give you good results; soy milk is best in this case, since it's the highest in protein.

Catching Drips in the Oven

Pies, and fruit pies especially, are notorious for bubbling up and over the confines of their pans. Those dastardly sticky fillings seem hell-bent on making their mark all over your clean oven. Don't let the pie win this fight! Although spillover can't be controlled, it can be contained. Every time you bake a pie, no matter how clean and dry it may appear, always place a large, rimmed baking sheet on the oven rack directly below it. This will catch any drips thrown overboard, and though it won't prevent them from burning during the baking process, it will save you the hassle of scrubbing out the oven later. It's much easier to clean a single baking sheet than a whole cavernous oven.

Substituting Frozen Fruit for Fresh

Cravings don't always follow the seasons, so the temptation to sneak in a blueberry pie in the middle of a January blizzard is completely understandable. While it is possible to use frozen fruits where fresh are called for, bear in mind that a pie is only as good as its ingredients, and nothing can compare to the flavor of ripe produce at the height of its growing season. There is also no direct conversion from fresh to frozen, since the freezing process creates many ice crystals inside the fruit which extract additional water when thawed. To prevent your pies from becoming a soupy mess, you must first fully thaw and drain the fruit. Only then can you measure and use it, although the weight will be different thanks to the water that was removed, so your best bet is to stick with volume measures. Otherwise, weigh out how much liquid you're removing once the fruit has thawed, and add in that same measurement of whole, thawed fruit, to equal the same final weight called for in the recipe.

Tenting with Aluminum Foil

Uneven baking is one of the most common perils of pie making. If your crust is already looking golden while the insides remain raw, it's time to employ a foil tent. It's easiest to assemble outside of the oven, so either prepare it before beginning to bake, or remove a par-baked pie from the oven before reinserting it with the tent intact. Drape a large piece of foil over the length of the pie, tucking the edges under the sides without crimping it down. You don't want the aluminum to actually seal or even touch the pie, but hover just above it to block the direct heat from continuing to brown the top. In the case of a single crust that's cooking too rapidly, tear off long rectangles of foil and place them just over the exposed edges. Since the foil is only loosely attached, be very careful moving your covered pie into the oven.

Storing and Saving Pies

Pies are like snowflakes; each one unique, and a fleeting image of beauty. Pies are considerably tastier than snowflakes, although they truly last about as long. They're made for sharing, not only because they contain a number of servings in one golden-brown package, but because they don't hold up well over time. The clock starts ticking the moment a pie comes out of the oven, hot and fresh and perfect. Fruit pies are best while still warm, deteriorating the fastest of any category. Even a day on the counter may be too long, as the juices seep into the crust, turning it into a soggy mess. To prolong its life as best you can, once completely cooled, place the whole pie under a cake dome, so that the dessert is covered but not sealed. The last thing you want to do is trap moisture in there, which will only speed up the degradation of the crust.

Chilled custard and cream pies can be covered in plastic wrap to prevent off-flavors lurking in the fridge from migrating into your dessert. The same goes for any frozen pies, which can be further wrapped in aluminum foil once solid, for longer storage. Be sure to label it clearly so that you don't forget what it is or when it was made! Frozen pies can keep for up to 3 months; custard and cream pies are generally best within 5 days; fruit pies should be eaten immediately, but can keep most of their original integrity for 2–3 days.

Fruit pies can also be revived, to a degree, by reheating them before serving. This crisps the crust once more in addition to making the perfect temperature contrast to a big scoop of ice cream. Tent your already baked pie with aluminum foil and place in a 350 degree preheated oven. Bake for approximately 10 minutes, until warm to the touch. Serve right away.

Freezing Unbaked Pies

What if you have a big event planned with lots of food to make, and a pie on the menu? You don't need to be rolling out dough as guests arrive—many pies can be prepared ahead of time and frozen. Simply follow the recipe right up until the point that it needs to be baked, then place the raw pie on a flat surface in the freezer instead. When you're ready to bake, preheat the oven as instructed and do not thaw the pie. Bake as per usual, but expect it to take an extra 20–40 minutes on top of the times stated.

PLEASE NOTE: Do not use a glass pie pan if you're planning on using this method! Moving it straight from the freezer to the oven can cause it to shatter. Stick with metal to be safe.

Toasting Nuts and Seeds

Many cooks recommend toasting nuts and seeds in the oven, but this isn't my method of choice. For one thing, why heat up the whole kitchen when you don't necessarily need the oven for the rest of your recipe? Secondly, I don't like the fact that I can't really watch over them or stir when necessary, which leads to horrifically blackened nuts far more often than I'd like to admit. Spare yourself the smoke and drama; try toasting over the stove instead.

Set a medium-sized skillet over moderate heat and toss in your nuts or seeds. Toast only 1–2 cups at a time, so that they can all get direct heat, thus cooking more evenly. It may start slowly, but once you start smelling that nutty aroma, things move quickly, so don't walk away from this process. Stir every minute or two, until the nuts or seeds are golden brown and highly aromatic. This will take anywhere from 7–15 minutes, depending on your particular variety. Immediately pour the contents of your skillet out onto a plate, to prevent continued cooking and subsequent burning.

Using Whole Vanilla Beans

There may be some killer vanilla extracts on the market these days, but there's still no liquid elixir that can touch the potent, sweet essence of a whole vanilla bean. You want to seek out plump, supple beans that bend easily without snapping. They should have a strong scent that carries a natural sweetness. Using them in your recipes is simple: Slit one bean lengthwise with a sharp knife and scrape out the tiny seeds within. Add those seeds to your mixture, and be thorough to extract every bit of bean you can.

For additional flavor, toss the spent vanilla bean pods into an ice cream base as well, to infuse, and then remove before churning. Personally, I prefer to save the pods instead in a container of granulated sugar to create incredible vanilla sugar, which does wonders as the top crust for crème brûlée.

Grinding Whole Spices

Ready-to-use, ground spices have their place and work quite well in most cases, but if you would just try grinding them from whole seeds to taste the difference, it may be hard to go back.

Using the same technique as you would to toast nuts over the stovetop, toast your whole spices first. This will bring out the aromatic and flavorful oils, allowing them to have a stronger and fuller taste. Just keep a very close eye on them, as they tend to toast very quickly; about 5–8 minutes should do it. They may not appear any different in color, but don't worry, you will definitely smell the difference. Let the spices cool completely before grinding down to a fine powder in a spice or coffee grinder. To achieve the finest consistency, you may want to first try freezing the spices. Measure out for your recipes only after completely ground, as whole spices measure very differently than powdered.

Thickening Cooked Custard

If I had a penny for every time I had a cauldron of bubbling non-dairy milk boil over and redecorate the kitchen. . . . Well, I think you know how the rest of that goes. It's not at all hard to thicken custards, puddings, or ice cream bases, but the key is that you must give them your undivided attention. Whisk vigorously before turning on the heat to break up any possible clumps hidden anywhere within the mixture, and then make sure that you never venture above medium heat. Medium-low is a better bet for the easily distracted, just as an extra measure of insurance.

Whisk occasionally at first, every few minutes, to ensure that nothing is sticking to or burning at the bottom of the pot. As bubbles begin to form around the edges, keep stirring constantly, with one hand hovering above the heat control. A rapid boil can quickly overflow the confines of any pot, so as soon as it's reached that stage, immediately kill the heat and move the whole pot off the burner. Keep whisking for a minute longer, to help facilitate the cooling process and ensure that no lumps form right at the end.

Straining Custards

Lumps happen, and that's a fact of life. They *don't* have to ruin your dessert, though! For the smoothest results possible, it's a good idea to strain every single cooked custard, to remove possible starchy clumps. Though technically an optional step, it's highly recommended. Use a fine-mesh sieve to filter out any offending particles, and try not to press the contents through with your spatula. Rather, tap on the side of the strainer firmly and rapidly to help gravity carry the custard through. Some bases are simply too thick to strain without a bit of additional pressure though, so you can use a spatula to help press the mixture through, if necessary. Discard any lumps you may catch.

Freezing Ice Creams and Sorbets without an Ice Cream Machine

Don't let the cost of a fancy ice cream maker stand in your way—strictly speaking, all you really need to make your own frozen treats is a reliable freezer and a vessel to contain your base of choice. The caveat is that the results simply won't be quite as smooth or creamy, and will take a bit more work on your part, but the flavors will be just as delicious.

Pour your chilled base into a large metal baking pan, about 13 x 9 inches, and set it on a flat, stable surface in your freezer. Now is not the time to try some fancy Tetris-style stacking on top of frozen bagged veggies, trust me! Give it at least 45–60 minutes in the deep freeze before opening the door again to check on it. Once the mixture begins to solidify around the edges, give the whole thing a vigorous whisk to break up any frozen chunks. Move the pan back into the freezer, and take another peek 30–45 minutes later. Whisk again, and repeat until the whole pan of ice cream is frozen to at least a soft-serve consistency. This can take anywhere from 2–4 hours, depending on the amount of ice cream and the temperature of your freezer.

Enjoy right away, or transfer into an airtight container and store in the freezer.

Caramelizing Crème Brûlée

After preparing and chilling the crème in question, use a paper towel to dab off any condensation or moisture that may have formed on the surface of the custard. Sprinkle sugar generously over the top, tilting the ramekin around so that the entire area is evenly covered; tap off any excess that doesn't stick.

If using a kitchen torch, start by holding the flame 3–4 inches away from the sugar, continuously moving the torch in a gentle circular motion. If you allow it to rest in one area for too long, you'll get uneven browning or worse, burning, so pay close attention to the flame. Slowly move in closer, until you start to see the granules liquefy. Keep on moving, turning the ramekin to reach all areas of the top, until all of the sugar has dissolved and turned a golden amber brown.

If brûléeing in the oven, position the oven rack at the very highest spot in the oven and turn on the broiler to high. When hot, place the ramekins directly under the broiler and let cook for 5–10 minutes, until the sugar has dissolved and is bubbling away. Rotate frequently to allow even browning.

Let the caramelized sugar rest for at least 5 minutes before serving, for it to set up to a hard crack. Completed crème brûlée can be stored in the refrigerator for no more than 30 minutes before the caramel begins to melt.

Making Vanilla Sugar

How can you improve upon an already stellar dessert? Vanilla sugar is the magic ingredient capable of turning the flavor up to 11. It makes the biggest difference in more delicately seasoned or simpler sweets where the addition is more detectable, but it adds a subtle something extra to anything it graces. Try it on top of crème brûlée, to sweeten whipped cream, or even in hot drinks, for starters. To make a practically unlimited supply, fill a jar of any size with standard granulated sugar. Every time you use a vanilla bean, jam the spent, dry pods right in the center. Over time, the vanilla will infuse its essence throughout the sugar, becoming stronger with age. Continue replenishing both the beans and sugar periodically, and you will always be prepared with some on hand.

TROUBLESHOOTING

My pastry is sticky and difficult to work with.

Pie crust is a very delicate balance of fat and flour, so it doesn't take much to throw that careful calibration off. As the fat warms, it becomes softer and looser, so keeping your cool is essential. Stop what you're doing and toss the dough back into the fridge for at least 30 minutes; you can speed things up by stashing it in the freezer for 15 minutes instead. If the pastry is already mostly or fully rolled out and now unwieldy, stick a flat metal sheet pan in the freezer for 15 minutes instead. Once icy to the touch, lay it directly on top of the dough, leaving it in place for 10–15 minutes. That should chill it enough to make the dough more manageable.

My pastry is really crumbly and won't hold together.

That one's a simple fix—you just need to add a tiny splash more water. Knead in about a teaspoon of ice-cold water at a time with your hands, until the dough is more cohesive.

Help! My dough stuck to the counter/rolling pin!

It's too late to easily solve this one now, but for future crusts, be a bit more generous with the flour. You want an even sprinkling of flour all over the area you plan to use, and a good margin of error beyond that as well. If you flip the disk of dough over at any point, flour whatever ends up as the top a second time, to prevent it from sticking to the rolling pin too.

To manage this problem if it's already happened, get an offset or flat cake frosting spatula and press it hard against the offending work surface. Using one smooth stroke, scrape it underneath the whole length of the dough, and it should come off in one piece. Re-flour thoroughly before resuming, and don't sweat the small stuff—any nicks or holes can be repaired later on.

The dough cracked/tore after I transferred it to the pan.

This is one of the most common and easily fixed issues you can encounter. The beautiful thing about pie crust is how infinitely malleable it is. Just grab some of the leftover scraps (or cut away some excess dough overhanging the sides of the pan) and press it into place. You can fill even the largest gaps this same way. If it refuses to stick, lightly moisten your fingers and dampen the edges of dough coming into contact. Press firmly to adhere, and then smooth out the results so that the entire crust is an even thickness.

My fruit filling is really runny.

Every new crop is a little bit different from the last, which means it's sometimes the luck of the draw that lands you with a batch of watery fruits. It's difficult to predict when this might happen, but if the fruit seems watery after you have sliced it, a quick toss in some additional cornstarch or arrowroot may be a wise preventative measure. In the most dire situations, you can stop the pie baking midway through, stir in a tablespoon or two of instant tapioca pearls, and return it to the oven. If it still needs more time to thicken than recommended in the recipe, tent it with foil to prevent the crust from over-baking.

The bottom crust came out soggy.

Another potential hazard of working with unpredictable fruit, the best you can do is try to anticipate this and lay down some insurance in advance. Sprinkle the bottom of the pie plate with about 1 tablespoon of cornstarch before easing in the dough, and then top that with an additional tablespoon once it's in place. This should at least help to absorb some of that excess liquid, rather than turning the crust itself into an edible sponge.

Ugh, my baked custard/cream pie has an ugly crack in the center.

Sounds like it was overcooked. It could be due to an oven that's too hot, or a baking time that's too long, so monitor both carefully. Most cracks can be covered with a generous topping of whipped cream, ice cream, fudge sauce, or fresh fruits, but a more gentle approach to the baking process can prevent it in the future. Turn down the temperature by about 25 degrees and bake the pie only until the edges appear set. Even if it still wobbles a bit in the center, it will continue to set up as it cools.

I always time it carefully, but my crust is still burning.

Home ovens are rarely calibrated properly, and on top of the natural temperature fluctuations, many have hot spots. Watch to see if just one side or area of the pie is baking faster than the others, and plan to rotate it periodically during the baking process if necessary. Always keep a second thermometer inside your oven to verify the temperature, since the digital read-out connected to the system is often inaccurate. Make sure that the racks are positioned in a way that the pie is firmly in the center of the oven, so that neither the top nor bottom is getting a stronger blast of heat. Finally, always keep a close eye on your pies and be ready to jump in with an aluminum foil tent, no matter how trusty your oven is.

My pie is all done, but the crust is still so pale/undercooked.

Not a problem at all! Just turn up the oven to 400 degrees and give it another 5–10 minutes. To ramp up the golden-brown goodness, brush it lightly with olive oil or a neutral vegetable oil before sending it back into the heat.

Once baked, my crust came out really tough, not flaky at all.

Sounds like the dough was overworked, either when you first created it, or when you went to roll it out. Try to handle it less next time, and leave larger pieces of margarine in the dough. The flaky texture is created when the margarine melts and leaves crisp pockets of baked flour behind. If you work those out before it ever hits the oven, you'll end up with something more closely related to an unleavened cracker.

There's a big gap between the filling and the top crust. What happened?

This is most commonly seen in fruit pies, because fruits shrink a bit as they bake and lose moisture. The top crust is pushed further away if it isn't properly vented, as the trapped steam puts upward pressure on it. This is merely an aesthetic issue, but can be mostly prevented with bigger decorative cut-outs, rather than skinny knife-drawn slits.

My meringue is really foamy/gooey/flat.

Meringue, even the eggless variety, is highly affected by the humidity in the air. On very humid summer days, depending on your climate, a meringue pie simply might not be the best choice to make.

After baking and cooling, the pie crust is sticking to the pan.

Pie crust naturally has enough fat to keep it from sticking to any vessel without additional lubrication required, but it can adhere itself to the pan for other reasons. Typically, it indicates that there is a hole or crack somewhere that was left unattended. As the filling baked, the sugars seeped out and caramelized between the pan and the crust, effectively adhering it. Simply be careful to check that there are no voids in the crust before piling in the filling, but if you're already stuck, the only thing that can be done is to run a thin knife all the way around the edge before trying to remove a slice.

I can never get a clean slice.

It's quite possible that this problem can be instantly fixed with a sharper knife. Unless you sharpen your knife before every use, there's a good chance that it's not performing at its peak capabilities. After slicing, switch over to a sturdy pie server that can support the full width of the slice. Don't fall for pie servers that come with a serrated edge built in; it's duller than a butter knife and guaranteed to mangle your pie. Additionally, make sure that the pie is completely cool before even thinking of removing a wedge, or else sacrifice those immaculately cut lines in favor of a still-warm, comfortingly gooey slice. Perfection is often overrated, you know.

CRUSTS AND
PASTRY
FOUNDATIONS

CLASSIC CRUST

Makes 1 or 2
Crusts

This "Old Reliable" is a baker's best friend, capable of standing and delivering anything loaded into it. It has stood by my side through thick and thin, gooey and gloppy, crunchy and chewy. The ingredients are nothing noteworthy—it's all a matter of how they're treated for the magic to happen. Keep everything, including bowls and utensils, as cold as possible so as not to melt the fat. Though a point of contention, I do adhere firmly to the belief that an all-"butter" crust is best. You may lose a little bit of flakiness, but the added flavor and crisp texture is worth that small sacrifice. For a lighter texture, feel free to sub out half of the margarine for pure vegetable shortening, and proceed as written otherwise. Do not be tempted to play around with coconut oil or any liquid oils in this one, as the structure simply isn't built for that kind of tinkering.

Even when I'm planning to make a single-crusted pie, I always use the double-crust proportions, to make the most of my time. The extra disk of dough can be frozen for up to 6 months with no harm, as long as it's thawed gradually in the fridge before use. That way, you're always prepared to whip up a pie at a moment's notice.

Two Crusts (For a Double-Crust):
2½ Cups All-Purpose Flour
2 Teaspoons Granulated Sugar
½ Teaspoon Salt
¾ Cup Non-Dairy Margarine,
    Chilled, Cut into Small Pieces
1 Tablespoon Lemon Juice

2–4 Tablespoons Ice-Cold Water

OR

Single Crust:
1¼ Cups All-Purpose Flour
1 Teaspoon Granulated Sugar

¼ Teaspoon Salt
6 Tablespoons Non-Dairy Margarine,
    Chilled, Cut into Small Pieces
1½ Teaspoons Lemon Juice
1–2 Tablespoons Ice-Cold Water

The easiest, quickest way to make a traditional pie crust is to get a helping hand from your food processor. Some say this approach sacrifices flakiness in favor of convenience, but I don't believe that any of my pies have suffered as a result. If you have the equipment, my advice is to use it! Place the flour, sugar, and salt in the bowl of your food processor and pulse to combine. Add the margarine and pulse 6–8 times, until the mixture resembles very coarsely ground almond meal. A few small chunks of margarine should remain visible, but nothing larger than the size of peas. Sprinkle lemon juice and the first tablespoon of water in while pulsing a few times to incorporate. If the dough holds together when squeezed, you're good to go. If it remains crumbly, keep adding water while pulsing, just a teaspoon at a time, until the dough is cohesive.

In case you don't have a food processor or just don't want to clean the darn thing afterward, the old-fashioned method is just as effective, if a bit more labor-intensive. Place the flour, sugar, and salt in a large bowl and use a pastry cutter or two forks to cut in the pieces of margarine. A few small chunks of margarine should remain visible, but nothing larger than the size of peas. Sprinkle lemon juice and one tablespoon of water into the bowl and stir well with a wide spatula. Sometimes it can be difficult to get the liquids properly incorporated, so it may be helpful to drop the formalities and just get in there to mix with your hands. If the dough holds together when squeezed, you're set. If it remains crumbly, keep adding water and mixing thoroughly, just a teaspoon at a time, until the dough is cohesive. Do your best not to over-mix or over-handle the dough, as this will make it tough when baked.

If making a double crust, divide the dough into two equal portions. Regardless of how many portions you now have, shape them into rough rounds and flatten them into disks about ½ inch in thickness. Wrap each tightly with plastic wrap and stash them in the fridge. Let chill for at least an hour, or up to a week. To save the unbaked dough even longer, store the pieces in your freezer for up to 6 months. (Don't forget to label them clearly!)

When you're ready to roll, lightly dust a clean, flat surface with an even coating of flour. Work on one disk of dough at a time, and coat both sides lightly with additional flour. Starting at the center of the disk, use your rolling pin to apply light pressure while rolling outwards to the edges. Try to maintain the round shape as best you can, turning the dough as needed. It may be helpful to periodically lift the dough to ensure that it's not adhering to the counter. Keep rolling until the dough extends at least 2 inches beyond the size of your pie pan all around.

Unless otherwise directed, carefully transfer the dough to a 9-inch pie pan, and crimp the edges or decorate to your heart's content. See page 24 for ideas. At the very least, trim away the excess dough so that only ½ inch is overhanging the lip of the pan. Tuck the extra dough underneath itself along the edge so that it's smooth.

For an unbaked crust, you're done here! Let the crust rest in the fridge while you prepare the filling. To blind-bake, see page 24 for the procedure.

If you're making pie with a top crust, roll out the second disk of dough in the same fashion as before, reapplying flour to the counter if need. Use cookie cutters to cut out decorative vents before moving the dough, or simply cut six vents with a sharp knife. Gently place the flattened dough onto the filled pie, centering it as best you can. Use kitchen shears or a sharp knife to trim the overhang to an inch. Tuck the excess from the top crust under the edge of the bottom piece of dough, pressing together firmly but gently to seal. Bake according to the recipe for the filling.

Chocolate Pastry Crust: Reduce the flour to 2⅓ cups and add ¼ cup Dutch-processed cocoa powder.

CORNMEAL CRUST

Makes 1 or 2 Crusts

The subtle sweetness found in corn makes this crust a complimentary foundation to dessert and dinner pies alike.

Two Crusts (For a Double-Crust):
2 Cups All-Purpose Flour
1 Cup Finely Ground White or
　Yellow Cornmeal
¾ Teaspoon Salt
1 Tablespoon Granulated Sugar
1 Cup Non-Dairy Margarine, Chilled,
　Cut into Small Pieces

¼–⅓ Cup Cold Water

OR

Single Crust:
1 Cup All-Purpose Flour
½ Cup Finely Ground White or
　Yellow Cornmeal
¼ Teaspoon Salt
1½ Teaspoons Granulated Sugar
½ Cup Non-Dairy Margarine,
　Chilled, Cut into Small Pieces
2–3 Tablespoons Cold Water

Place the flour, cornmeal, salt, and sugar in the food processor and pulse to combine. Add the margarine and pulse 6–8 times, until the mixture resembles very coarsely ground almond meal. A few small chunks of margarine should remain visible, but nothing larger than the size of peas. Sprinkle in the first two tablespoons of water while pulsing a few times to incorporate. If the dough holds together when squeezed, you're good to go. If it remains crumbly, keep adding water while pulsing, just a teaspoon at a time, until the dough is cohesive.

Alternatively, for those without a food processor, place the flour, cornmeal, salt, and sugar in a large bowl and use a pastry cutter or two forks to cut in the pieces of margarine. A few small chunks of margarine should remain visible, but nothing larger than the size of peas. Sprinkle the first two tablespoons of water into the bowl and stir well with a wide spatula. Sometimes it can be difficult to get the liquids properly incorporated, so it may be helpful to drop the formalities and just get in there to mix with your hands. If the dough holds together when squeezed, you're set. If it remains crumbly, keep adding water and mixing thoroughly, just a teaspoon at a time, until the dough is cohesive. Do your best not to over-mix or over-handle the dough, as this will make it tough when baked.

If making a double crust, divide the dough into two equal portions. Regardless of how many portions you now have, shape them into rough rounds and flatten them into disks about ½ inch in thickness. Wrap each tightly with plastic wrap and stash them in the fridge. Let chill for at least an hour, or up to a week. To save the unbaked dough even longer, store the pieces in your freezer for up to 6 months. (Don't forget to label them clearly!)

When you're ready to roll, lightly dust a clean, flat surface with an even coating of flour. Work on one disk of dough at a time, and coat both sides lightly with additional flour. Starting at the center of the disk, use your rolling pin to apply light pressure while rolling outwards to the edges. Try to maintain the round shape as best as you can, turning the dough as needed. It may be helpful to periodically lift the dough to ensure that it's not adhering to the counter. Keep rolling until the dough extends at least 2 inches beyond the size of your pie pan all around.

Unless otherwise directed, carefully transfer the dough to your pie pan, and crimp the edges or decorate as desired. See page 23 for guidance. At the very least, trim away the excess dough so that only ½ inch is overhanging the lip of the pan. Tuck the extra dough underneath itself along the edge so that it's smooth.

For an unbaked crust, you're done here! Let the crust rest in the fridge while you prepare the filling. To blind-bake, see page 24 for the procedure.

If you're making pie with a top crust, roll out the second disk of dough in the same fashion as before, reapplying flour to the counter if need. Use cookie cutters to cut out decorative vents before moving the dough, or simply cut six vents with a sharp knife. Gently place the flattened disk onto the filled pie, centering it as best you can. Use kitchen shears or a sharp knife to trim the overhang to an inch. Tuck the excess from the top crust under the edge of the bottom piece of dough, pressing together firmly but gently to seal. Bake according to the recipe for the filling.

Rye Crust: Use rye flour instead of cornmeal and add 1 teaspoon whole caraway seeds.

Semolina Crust: Use semolina flour instead of cornmeal and reduce the sugar to 1 teaspoon.

CRUNCHY CEREAL CRUSTS

*Makes 12
Personal Pie
Crusts*

Designed purely with nutrition in mind, crunchy nugget cereals don't get a whole lot of love. Just asking about what others call them, I got back a whole range of creative responses, the best of which being "squirrel nibbles" and "sawdust." For such utilitarian eats, they sure do make for incredible pie crust fodder. While the standard pastry can become a bit tiresome, this is the sort of shell that I could happily eat plain, unfilled. Finally, the humble whole grain cereal just might get some respect for this downright delicious showing.

3 Cups Whole Grain Nugget Cereal,
  Such as Grape-Nuts®
2 Tablespoons Cornstarch

¼ Cup Granulated Sugar
⅛ Teaspoon Salt

6 Tablespoons Non-Dairy Margarine,
  Melted
Up to 1 Tablespoon Water, if Needed

Preheat your oven to 350 degrees and lightly grease 12 regular-sized muffin tins. While the oven comes up to temperature, prepare the crust by first placing the cereal, cornstarch, sugar, and salt in your food processor. Pulse repeatedly to pulverize the cereal bits into a fine powder. The mixture won't hold together as well if the meal is still coarse, so really let those nuggets have it!

Once it looks pretty much like regular flour, begin slowly drizzling in the melted margarine. Continue pulsing to incorporate, until thoroughly moistened and the mixture holds together when pressed. If it still seems a bit dry, add up to 1 tablespoon of water.

Distribute equal scoops of the loose crust into your prepared muffin cups. Use your fingers to press it evenly up the sides and across the bottoms, taking care to fill any gaps.

Bake for 10–12 minutes, until just lightly browned and no longer wet to the touch. Let cool completely before filling or removing from the pan.

GLUTEN-FREE CRUST

Makes 1 Bottom Crust

Pie is a dessert meant for sharing, so it breaks my heart to think that anyone might be left out of that sweet communal experience. For my gluten-free friends, fear not: This is but one of many options that are a bit easier to digest. Though not flaky like traditional crust, it's actually a whole lot easier, so new bakers may be more comfortable starting with this simple foundation. Rather than rolling out a big sheet of dough, the raw mixture is merely pressed into place before baking. As long as you keep it cold, it's as close to fool-proof as you can get in the art of pie-making. For those who need to mind their gluten, this can be seamlessly swapped in for any recipe that calls for a classic crust on the bottom.

1 Cup Mochiko
¼ Cup Tapioca Flour
1½ Teaspoons Whole Flaxseeds, Ground

1½ Teaspoons Granulated Sugar
½ Teaspoon Xanthan Gum
¼ Teaspoon Salt

6 Tablespoons Non-Dairy Margarine, Chilled
½ Teaspoon Apple Cider Vinegar
2–3 Tablespoons Cold Water

Break out your food processor, and after installing the blade, begin loading the dry goods into the bowl. Add the mochiko and tapioca flour first, along with the ground flaxseeds, sugar, xanthan gum, and salt. Pulse briefly to combine.

Cut the margarine into tablespoon-sized pieces and pulse again, breaking it down into a coarse crumb-like mixture. There should still be small pieces of the margarine visible, so don't go crazy and allow it to completely blend in. Add the vinegar and the first two tablespoons of water, pulsing to incorporate. Slowly drizzle in additional water while pulsing the machine, just until the mixture comes together as a cohesive dough. Be patient, giving the flours plenty of time to hydrate before adding in the next splash of water, to ensure that you don't end up with wet sludge.

Press the dough together into one flat round about ½ inch thick. Wrap it up in a piece of plastic wrap and stash the raw crust in your fridge for at least 20 minutes before proceeding.

When you're ready to bake, unwrap the disk of chilled dough and place it in your desired pie pan. Use the palms of your hands to press it out into the bottom of the baking dish, coaxing it up the sides, and filling in any empty space. You can use the bottom of a flat drinking glass or measuring cup to further smooth the surface after the entire area is evenly covered. Proceed with the pie recipe from here on out, or return the shaped crust to the fridge for up to a day.

To blind-bake the crust, see page 24 for tips.

(NOTE: Cannot be used for upper crusts)

GRAHAM CRACKER OR COOKIE CRUST

**Makes 1
Crust**

Using a cookie crust for a pie is like getting two desserts in one forkful, which is why I love them so much. There are always some cookies, crackers, or crumbs on hand in my house, so I resort to this quick trick more often than I'd like to admit. Feel free to keep experimenting with new ingredients; finely crushed pretzels or chips make for a delightfully salty contrast to many sweet fillings.

1¾ Cups Graham Cracker Crumbs
   (page 48 or Store-Bought; About
   14 Full Rectangle Crackers)

4–5 Tablespoons Non-Dairy
   Margarine or Coconut Oil, Melted

For a baked crust, preheat your oven to 350 degrees. Otherwise, don't touch that oven!

For the best texture, be sure to pulse your cookie of choice in a food processor until very finely ground. The resulting crumbs should be about the consistency of coarse almond meal. Pick out any larger pieces and re-process as needed.

Drizzle the melted margarine or coconut oil into the crumbs, and stir thoroughly to coat everything evenly. The mixture shouldn't be wet, but just moist, and capable of sticking together when pressed.

Transfer the mix to a 9-inch or 10-inch round pie pan, and use lightly dampened fingers to firmly press it down on the bottom and along the sides. Use the bottom of a flat measuring cup or drinking glass for smoother surfaces. If using a 9-inch pan, you may have more crumbs than needed, so feel free to remove the excess and either save it for future crusts, or bake separately on a flat baking sheet to create any easy sweet ice cream topping.

Use as is, or bake the lined pie pan for 10 minutes, until golden.

Vanilla Cookie Crust: Use vanilla cookie crumbs instead of the graham cracker crumbs (see page 48 for homemade options).

Chocolate Cookie Crust: Use chocolate cookie crumbs instead of the graham cracker crumbs (see page 48 for homemade options).

Ice Cream Cone Crust: Use smashed sugar cones instead of the graham cracker crumbs.

RAWESOME FRUIT AND NUT CRUST

Makes 1 Pie Crust

Closely related in content to raw energy bars, this sweet and nutty base stays soft and chewy, even when frozen. An excellent candidate for any pie that doesn't go into the oven, it's just as delicious when used with cooked fillings.

¾ Cup Coconut Flour   ¾ Cup Raisins   ¼–⅓ Cup Water
¾ Cup Almond Meal   Pinch Salt

Pull out your food processor and place the coconut flour, almond meal, raisins, and salt in the work bowl. Pulse until the raisins break down fairly smoothly and the mixture becomes sticky and only slightly coarse. Drizzle in the water, a few teaspoons at a time, pulsing until crust mixture holds together in a big clump. Pulse very thoroughly after each splash of water, pausing to scrape down the sides of the bowl as needed, to make sure you don't add too much liquid.

Transfer the sticky dough to an ungreased pie pan and use lightly moistened fingers to press it evenly up the sides and across the bottom. Keep chilled until ready to use.

The raw crust, once pressed into a pan, can be wrapped tightly in plastic wrap and frozen for up to a month if desired. Simply thaw for at least 1 hour at room temperature before filling.

> If you find you have more of the mixture than you need to line your pie pan, you can press the excess into walnut-sized balls for instant snack bites! Feel free to mix in finely chopped chocolate to sweeten the deal further, and store in an airtight container in the fridge for up to a week.

> Switch it up! Try different complimentary flavors (or utilize ingredients you already have on hand) by swapping out the almond meal for finely ground pecans or walnuts, or substitute dates or dried figs for raisins.

WHOLESOME WHOLE WHEAT CRUST

*Makes 1 or 2
Crusts*

When you want a crust with character but that will still play nicely with others, this hearty little number won't disappoint. Especially well suited to savory applications, the additional fiber and protein of the germ and bran of the whole wheat kernel will provide an excellent excuse to eat any pie for dinner.

Two Crusts (For a Double-Crust Pie):

1⅓ Cups White Whole Wheat or Whole Wheat Pastry Flour

⅔ Cup Whole Wheat Flour

¾ Teaspoon Salt

½ Cup Olive Oil

1½ Teaspoons Apple Cider Vinegar

2–4 Tablespoons Cold Water

OR

Single Crust:

⅔ Cup White Whole Wheat or Whole Wheat Pastry Flour

⅓ Cup Whole Wheat Flour

½ Teaspoon Salt

¼ Cup Olive Oil

1 Teaspoon Apple Cider Vinegar

1–2 Tablespoons Cold Water

In a large bowl, mix together both flours and salt. Add in the oil and vinegar at the same time, and stir with a wide spatula until the dough begins to come together. Drizzle in just about a teaspoon of water at a time, until you have a stiff, cohesive dough. Be careful not to go overboard with the liquid, as it should still be thick enough to happily roll out. It may take some serious elbow grease to bring together this mixture, so if you have a stand mixer, this would be a good time to use it instead.

If preparing a double crust, divide the dough into two equal rounds, wrapping one up in plastic wrap and placing in the fridge to chill. You'll return to it for the top crust later on.

On a lightly floured surface, use a rolling pin to roll the dough out to an even round about ⅛-inch thick. Unless otherwise directed, transfer the dough to a 9-inch round pie pan and trim the excess around the edges. Chill until ready to use or blind-bake (page 24).

ACCOMPANIMENTS & COMPONENTS

CHOCOLATE COOKIE CRUMBS

*Makes About
2 Scant Cups
Finely Ground
Crumbs*

A simple crumb-based crust is only as good as the cookies it's made from, meaning that quality really counts here. It's a good sign when friends walk into your kitchen and demand to know what smells so good, when it's only the plain crust in the oven! If you can't secure flavorful store-bought wafer cookies, suddenly find your stash has run low, or simply want to create your treats completely from scratch, the DIY alternative is easier than it may sound. Rather than painstakingly shaping each biscuit, this formula yields a loose, crisp crumb mixture that needs little further persuasion to reach the ideal pie crust consistency. In fact, after measuring the proper amount of crumbs for your desired crust, you can put them right back into the food processor and use the pulse function to incorporate the melted margarine called for in the recipe (page 48). You're well on your way to pie perfection from there.

1 Cup All-Purpose Flour
1 Teaspoon Cornstarch
½ Cup Granulated Sugar

⅓ Cup Cocoa Powder
½ Teaspoon Salt

6 Tablespoons Non-Dairy Margarine,
Melted

Preheat your oven to 300 degrees and line a baking sheet with a piece of parchment paper or a silpat.

Combine the flour, cornstarch, sugar, cocoa powder, and salt in the bowl of your stand mixer fitted with a paddle attachment. Mix on low speed until all the ingredients are well blended. Drizzle in the melted margarine while the mixer runs on low, until the mixture is thoroughly moistened and clumps together in small clusters. Scrape down the sides of the bowl to double-check that there are no remaining pockets of dry ingredients before proceeding.

Spread the coarse crumbs on your prepared sheet pan. Bake for 28–32 minutes, until no longer shiny and the crumbs around the edges have darkened slightly. Remove from the oven and let the crumbs cool completely on the sheet pan.

Before using in your next pie masterpiece, toss the whole batch of baked crumbs into your food processor and pulse until finely ground. Now you're ready to start baking again!

Graham Cracker Crumbs: Omit the cornstarch and swap the cocoa out for an equal measure of graham flour.
Vanilla Cookie Crumbs: Omit the cocoa powder, increase the flour to 1⅓ cups total, and add 1 teaspoon vanilla extract.

COCONUT BACON

Makes 2 Cups

One would never guess that such unassuming ingredients combined in the right proportions would bear such uncanny resemblance to crispy, smoky bacon bits. In fact, the first time that distinctive aroma wafted from the oven, my meat-eating mother asked why it "suddenly smelled like salami in the kitchen." For once, I'll take that as a compliment! These coconut bacon pieces are so addictive that I often make a double batch to accommodate random snack cravings in addition to what's called for in a particular recipe. Simply distribute the mixture between two separate baking dishes instead of one.

3 Tablespoons Soy Sauce
1 Tablespoon Liquid Smoke

1 Tablespoon Maple Syrup
1 Tablespoon Olive Oil

⅛ Teaspoon Ground Black Pepper
2 Cups Coconut Flakes

Preheat your oven to 300 degrees and set aside a 9 x 13-inch baking pan.

Stir together the soy sauce, liquid smoke, maple syrup, oil, and pepper in a large mixing bowl. Toss the coconut in and stir with a wide spatula, coating the flakes thoroughly with the liquids. Be gentle to prevent the coconut from breaking into smaller pieces.

Pour everything, including the marinade, into your waiting pan. Bake for about 28–32 minutes, stirring every 10 minutes or so to keep the entire batch cooking evenly. The flakes can burn very easily and surprisingly quickly, so stand by and keep a close eye on it the entire time it's in the oven.

Cook until golden brown all over and highly aromatic. Be aware that your kitchen may smell like bacon for the rest of the day, but I would hardly consider that a problem. Straight out of the oven, the bacon will still be slightly soft to the touch but will crisp up nicely once cool.

Let cool completely and store at room temperature in an airtight container. The bacon will keep for up to two weeks in a dark, cool place.

COCONUT WHIPPED CREAM

*Makes About
3 Cups*

A dollop of freshly whipped cream tops off any treat with added flair! Next time you find yourself with a lackluster treat, try dressing it up with a spoonful of the white fluffy stuff and see what a difference it makes. Even if it's a cereal bar, I say it can be improved with whipped cream on the side. Between rich coconut milk and heavy cream, there's no competition: coconut wins every time. With a subtle flavor all its own, coconut contributes additional interest to any plate without stealing the show. It really does play well with others. Keep a can of full-fat coconut milk in your fridge at all times, so you're prepared to dress up any grand finale, be it decent, good, or truly great.

1 (14 Ounce) Can Full-Fat Coconut
   Milk

1–2 Tablespoons Granulated Sugar
½ Teaspoon Vanilla Extract

It takes some advanced planning to get the fluffiest whipped cream out of coconut milk, but your patience will pay off. Begin by placing the can of coconut milk in the fridge and allow it to sit overnight or at least 8 hours. This solidifies the coconut cream, which is the part that we want here.

After a nice, long chill, carefully remove the lid, without shaking or turning the can upside-down. Scoop out the opaque white cream on top and place in the bowl of your stand mixer, leaving the clear water at the bottom. The water can't be whipped, but don't discard it—it's fantastic in smoothies, curries, and many other recipes!

Returning your attention to the cream, fit your mixer with the whip attachment. Begin beating on low speed and increase gradually until you reach the highest speed setting. Slowly sprinkle in the sugar while the motor runs, followed by the vanilla. Add enough sugar to satisfy your own sweet tooth. I prefer less to contrast with the sweetness of the pie or other dessert, but it's up to your discretion.

Continue whipping for about 5 minutes until the mixture is light and fluffy. Use one whole batch to top a single pie, or garnish many single servings.

Easy as Vegan Pie

MERINGUE

Meringue pies have long been merely the stuff of legend within the vegan community, but no more. Bring them back into real life with ease, or just enjoy the feathery topping solo as meringue kiss cookies. This is one of the rare times that I must insist on using a specific brand of egg replacer, as it's the only one proven to work every single time. Bear in mind that while it is more stable than an egg white-based meringue, the recipe is still vulnerable to humidity, so try to avoid making it on the hottest, stickiest days of summer, to ensure the best results.

⅓ Cup Ener-G Egg Replacer®   ½ Cup Granulated Sugar
¾ Cup Water   1 Teaspoon Vanilla Paste or Extract

To top a pie, make sure that your pie is fully baked and cool to the touch before preheating your oven to 300 degrees.

To make meringue cookies, preheat your oven to 225 degrees and line two baking sheets with silpats or parchment paper.

Combine the egg replacer with the water in your stand mixer fitted with the whisk attachment, and turn it up to the highest setting, whipping the mixture for a full 5 minutes. At that time, begin to slowly sprinkle in the sugar, and proceed to whip for 5 more minutes. It will have substantially increased in volume at this point, making for a light and fluffy concoction, much like whipped cream. Scrape down the sides of the bowl, remove any excess batter from the beater, and gently fold in the vanilla with a wide spatula.

For pie topping, smooth the entire batch of meringue, whipped to stiff peaks, over the surface of the pie, heaping it slightly towards the center. Use a flat spatula to add ripples or waves, gently massaging the meringue as desired. Alternately, flick the spatula gently across the surface to create short spikes. Place the pie on the top rack of your oven with the broiler set to high, rotating the pie every minute or two for even browning. Once all the tips of the meringue are golden, quickly remove the pie and serve right away.

To make cookies, either transfer the meringue to a piping bag and pipe swirls, or use two spoons to drop dollops of the fluff on baking sheets. Aim for something about the size of a golf ball. You don't need to leave a whole lot of space between cookies because they shouldn't spread, but make sure they still have some room to breathe. Bake for 50–60 minutes until they no longer look shiny, but you do not want them to brown at all. Turn off the oven, but leave the meringues inside until the oven fan shuts itself off, in order to further dry the cookies to a crispy texture. Once cool, store in an airtight container at room temperature, for up to a week.

PEPITA PARM

Makes 2 Cups

Just a sprinkle will do! Instantly kick up savory dishes from salad to pasta with a little pinch of "parmesan." Adding a gently salty, umami quality that punches up flavors to the next level, I always have a jar on hand. Stash it in the freezer and keep it around at all times.

1 Cup Raw Pepitas (Shelled Pumpkin Seeds)
1 Teaspoon Salt
1 Teaspoon Onion Powder

2 Tablespoons Whole Flaxseeds, Ground
½ Cup Nutritional Yeast

1 Tablespoon Chickpea Miso or Sweet White Miso Paste
1 Teaspoon Rice Vinegar

Place all of the ingredients in your food processor and pulse repeatedly in short bursts. Pause to scrape down the sides of the bowl as needed to incorporate any scraps that may be eluding the blade. Continue until the mixture has a coarse, crumbly, yet consistent texture and parmesan-like appearance. Store in an airtight container in the fridge for up to 2 weeks.

SALTED CHOCOLATE FUDGE SAUCE

Makes About
1½ Cups

More than merely an ice cream parlor cure-all, covering up a multitude of flavor sins, proper hot fudge is capable of complimenting, rather than obscuring, a wide variety of desserts. Though the amount of salt used to make the chocolate sing may appear excessive at first glance, you won't even notice it once the fudge is complete and adorning your pies. All you'll taste is quite possibly the best hot fudge sauce you've encountered yet.

¼ Cup Dutch-Processed Cocoa Powder
¼ Cup Granulated Sugar
⅔ Cup Plain Non-Dairy Milk

½ Cup Light Corn Syrup or Brown Rice Syrup*
½ Teaspoon Coarse Sea Salt

6 Ounces (1 Cup) Semi-Sweet Chocolate Chips
2 Tablespoons Non-Dairy Margarine
1 Teaspoon Vanilla Extract

In a small saucepan, first whisk the cocoa powder and sugar together, breaking up any lumps of cocoa and dispersing it evenly throughout the granules. Slowly drizzle in the non-dairy milk in a steady stream while whisking, incorporating the dry goods. It may take a moment to convince the cocoa to mix smoothly into the mixture, so plan to keep whisking for another couple of minutes before pouring in the corn or brown rice syrup next. Add the salt and set over moderate heat. Stir continuously, scraping along the bottom and sides of the pot to make sure that nothing sticks or scalds.

When the liquid reaches a rolling boil, immediately turn off the heat and drop in both the chocolate chips and margarine. Keep stirring, using the residual heat to melt them in smoothly. Finally, incorporate the vanilla.

Let cool for at least 15 minutes to use as hot fudge, or transfer to heat-safe jars to store for later. Cool completely before covering and storing in the fridge. The sauce with thicken significantly once chilled, but reheats beautifully after just 30–60 seconds in the microwave.

*For an added layer of flavor, using malted barley syrup instead of corn or brown rice syrup will incorporate a subtle touch of nuttiness.

SPECULOOS COOKIES

Crisp like gingersnaps but redolent of cinnamon rather than ginger, these brown sugar cookies can be spiced heavily or lightly, rolled thick or thin, and used as an ingredient or finished treat. Endlessly versatile, no two bakers' speculoos will taste the same, so consider this your invitation to tinker with the taste as desired. Additional spices add complexity here, but in a pinch, cinnamon alone will certainly do the trick. Largely considered a holiday cookie, their solid construction makes them an ideal candidate for long storage periods and rough shipping as gifts to loved ones abroad.

3 Cups All-Purpose Flour
1 Tablespoon Whole Flaxseeds,
    Ground
1 Tablespoon Ground Cinnamon
¼ Teaspoon Ground Cloves

¼ Teaspoon Ground Allspice
¼ Teaspoon Salt
¼ Teaspoon Baking Soda
½ Cup Non-Dairy Margarine

1 Cup Dark Brown Sugar, Firmly
    Packed
1 Tablespoon Molasses
4 Tablespoons Water

Preheat your oven to 300 degrees.

In either a large metal bowl or a stand mixer, whisk together the flour, ground flaxseeds, spices, baking soda, and salt. While you can certainly bring this dough together by hand, it will require some vigorous stirring, so I would advise bringing out the heavy artillery if you have it!

Meanwhile, combine the margarine, sugar, and molasses in a small saucepan and heat gently. Cook the mixture and stir gently, just until the margarine has melted and the sugar is completely dissolved. Pour the hot liquid into the bowl of dry ingredients, immediately followed by the water, and mix well. It will be very thick and somewhat difficult to mix, but give it all you've got and don't waste time—it will become even firmer as it cools.

Turn out the dough onto a lightly floured surface, press it into a ball, and roll it out to about ⅛ inch thick. Cut it into your desired shapes with cookie cutters and transfer the cookies over to a silpat. Simple rectangles are my favorites in this case, which are made with evenly spaced cuts using a scalloped pastry wheel. To replicate the embossed pattern pictured, use an immaculately clean rubber stamp of any sort to press into the surface of the raw dough. I like to stick with the seasonal theme and use various snowflakes.

Bake 13–20 minutes, depending on the size of your shapes, until the edges of your cookies are just barely browned. Let the cookies sit for a minute on the baking sheet before moving them over to a wire rack to cool.

Store in an airtight container at room temperature for up to 2 weeks, or in the freezer for 6 months.

Yield varies depending on the cookie cutter.

SPECULOOS SPREAD

*Makes 1
Generous Cup*

Gaining popularity in the States well before the cookie itself, the best way to describe speculoos spread is to imagine if peanut butter were made of cookies rather than nuts. Velvety smooth, mildly flavored, and sweet as frosting, you'd be hard pressed to include it as part of a balanced breakfast. Something about the commercial variety just never struck my fancy, seeming both waxy and pasty at the same time, with too little flavor payoff to make the consistency worth suffering through. Sure, my homemade rendition has a bit more grit and crunch to it, but I like to think of that as much-needed character in a textural wasteland. Plus, avoiding all the questionable oils and stabilizers is a nice added bonus.

5 Ounces Speculoos Cookies (About 1¼ Cups Finely Ground) (page 60)

¼ Cup Non-Dairy Margarine or Coconut Oil, Melted
1 Tablespoon Light Corn Syrup or Light Agave Nectar

2 Tablespoons Vegan Cream Cheese

Lightly smash the cookies into smaller pieces to make them easier to break down, before placing them in your food processor. Pulse until they are very fine crumbs. Add the "cream cheese" and syrup, pulse to combine, and then allow the motor to run. Slowly stream in the margarine or coconut oil. After incorporating all of the oil, pause to scrape down the sides of the bowl, and then puree for about 2–3 minutes more to make sure the mixture is fully emulsified and smooth.

Store in an airtight container at room temperature for up to a week, or in the fridge for up to three weeks. Once chilled, the spread will solidify, but softens up nicely after just a few seconds in the microwave.

TRIPLE VANILLA ICE CREAM

*Makes 1
Scant Quart*

Fresh out of the oven and still bubbling slightly around the edges, warm fruit pies are one of life's greatest pleasures. Nothing compares to breaking that golden, flaky crust and releasing a plume of sweet aromas from within. The only thing that would make that moment better is a soft scoop of vanilla ice cream, melting on top, mingling with the juices to create a creamy sauce. Quality vanilla makes all the difference in the world, since it's front and center in this simple ice cream base, so don't be tempted to cut corners.

2 Cups Vanilla Non-Dairy Milk
1½ Tablespoons Arrowroot
1½ Teaspoons Cornstarch

½ Cup Granulated Sugar
¼ Teaspoon Salt
1 Whole Vanilla Bean

1 Teaspoon Vanilla Extract
3 Tablespoons Non-Dairy Margarine

In a medium saucepan, whisk together the non-dairy milk, arrowroot, cornstarch, sugar, and salt while the liquid is still cold, beating vigorously to ensure that there are no remaining clumps. Use a knife to split the vanilla bean down the middle and scrape out the seeds. Toss both the seeds and spent pods into the pan.

Set the mixture over medium heat, whisking continuously until it comes to a boil. Immediately turn off the heat and carefully remove the pods. Don't throw them out; they can be washed off, dried, and placed in a container of sugar to make vanilla sugar.

While the custard is still hot, whisk in the margarine and stir until it has fully melted and become seamlessly incorporated. Let chill completely in the refrigerator before proceeding.

The custard will be very thick once chilled, so be sure to whisk vigorously, or give it a quick spin in the blender before churning in your ice cream maker according to the manufacturer's instructions.

Transfer the soft ice cream into an airtight container and let it rest in the freezer for at least 3 hours before serving, or until solid enough to scoop.

VEGAN HONEY-FLAVORED SYRUP

*Makes About
1¼ Cups*

When plain old agave just won't do, this bee-free "honey" imposter is close enough to actual flower nectar that hive dwellers might confuse it for their own work. Even if you have no plans to use it in your baked goods, it's a delicious condiment to have on hand for tea, pancakes, or scones.

1½ Cups Granulated Sugar

⅛ Teaspoon Alum (Optional)

½ Cup Water

¼ Cup Amber Agave Nectar

½ Teaspoon Lemon Juice

⅓ Cup Dried, Untreated Rose Petals,
   or 1 Cup Fresh

¼ Teaspoon Orange Blossom Water

¼ Teaspoon Vanilla Extract

In a medium saucepan, combine the sugar, alum (if using), water, agave, and lemon juice, and bring to a boil. Reduce the heat so that the mixture maintains a gentle simmer for 10 minutes.

Meanwhile, if using fresh rose petals, thoroughly rinse and dry them, being careful to remove any rotten or green sections.

Remove the pan from the stove and add in the rose petals. Stir to incorporate, cover, and let steep for 45–60 minutes.

Strain out the spent petals (or just fish them out with a fork if they're easily removed) and mix in the orange blossom water and vanilla. Transfer to a glass jar and let cool completely before covering. Store in a dark place at room temperature.

The "honey" will keep almost indefinitely, but will begin to lose its delicate floral flavor after 6 months.

CUSTARD, CREAM, AND PUDDING PIES

ADZUKI BEAN PIE

Makes 8–10 Servings

It was during my very first trip to Japan, at 10 years old, when I first encountered beans served for dessert. Sandwiched between two soft, pancake-like cookies, that single *dorayaki* flipped my clearly divided world of sweet and savory on its head. Sadly unappreciated in Western cultures, sweetened adzuki beans are far more delicious than their humble legume origins may suggest. Toothsome and satisfyingly starchy, they're more filling that mere candy, but are sweet enough to easily fit into that same category. Blended up into an impossibly creamy custard, this filling is delicious either perfectly silky smooth or left with a bit more texture.

1 Unbaked Classic Crust (page 36) or Wholesome Whole Wheat Crust (page 44)
2 Cups Cooked Adzuki Beans, Divided

6 Ounces (½ Aseptic Package) Extra-Firm Silken Tofu
¼ Cup Plain Non-Dairy Milk
½ Cup Dark Brown Sugar, Firmly Packed

½ Cup Granulated Sugar
2 Tablespoons Cornstarch
1 Teaspoon Vanilla Extract
¼ Teaspoon Ground Cinnamon
¼ Teaspoon Salt

Preheat your oven to 350 degrees.

Place 1½ cups of the cooked beans in your food processor or blender, along with the tofu, non-dairy milk, both types of sugar, cornstarch, vanilla, cinnamon, and salt. Thoroughly puree, pausing to scrape down the sides of the container periodically, until the entire mixture is silky smooth. Stir in the reserved ½ cup of adzuki beans with a spatula, so as not to break them up. They will add a nice bit of texture throughout the filling, and using the machine to pulse them would make the pie gritty instead.

Pour the mixture into your unbaked pie crust, and smooth down the top. Place the filled pie pan on a baking sheet for easier retrieval from the oven, and decorate the edges with additional pie crust if desired. For the pie shown, scraps of dough were cut into flower shapes, brushed with water on the bottom, and firmly attached to the edge of the crust.

Bake for 40–50 minutes, until crust is golden brown and the filling is set around the edges, but still slightly wobbly in the center, much like a cheesecake. Let cool completely and then chill for at least 2 hours before slicing and serving. Top with fresh berries and/or coconut whipped cream (page 52) for a lighter, brighter dessert.

BANANA TAPIOCA PUDDING PIE

Makes 8–12 Servings

Even when you can't recall buying bananas recently, it seems there's always a bunch sitting on the kitchen counter, threatening to ripen to an unappealing shade of brown-black at the drop of a hat. Assertive in their desire to be consumed, the mere scent of them can drive typically reasonable cooks into a banana bread baking frenzy. As much as I love the classic quick bread, one can only take so much of it when bundle after bundle of bananas demands to be used. Before the situation becomes dire, catch those perfectly ripe, still slightly firm fruits and think outside the loaf pan. Shying away from a straightforward pudding pie, tapioca adds a delightful toothsome texture, making every bite worth savoring.

1 Blind-Baked Vanilla Wafer Cookie
   Crust (page 48)
Banana Layer:
3 Medium or 2 Large Bananas, Cut
   into ¼-Inch Slices
2 Tablespoons Lemon Juice

Vanilla Tapioca Pudding:
½ Cup Small Pearl Tapioca (Not
   Instant)
2½ Cups Plain Non-Dairy Milk,
   Divided
⅔ Cup Granulated Sugar
¼ Cup Cornstarch
¼ Teaspoon Salt

2 Tablespoons Non-Dairy Margarine
½ Whole Vanilla Bean, Split and
   Scraped, or 2 Teaspoons Vanilla
   Extract
To Finish:
1 Batch Whipped Coconut Cream
   (page 52)
1 Medium Banana, Thinly Sliced

This pie does require a bit of advanced planning, so make sure you factor the timing into your schedule before embarking on this delicious journey. First, you'll need to cover the tapioca pearls with 1 cup of the non-dairy milk for at least 3 hours at room temperature. Alternately, you can soak them overnight in the fridge to expedite the process in the morning.

In a small bowl, toss the banana slices with lemon juice to coat, then evenly distribute over the prepared crust and set aside. Discard any excess lemon juice. Set aside for the time being.

In a medium saucepan, add 1 more cup of the "milk" along with the tapioca and any of the remaining soaking liquid as well. Set over medium heat, stirring gently but constantly as the mixture comes up to a boil. It might not be a rapid-fire thrill ride, but you must stay vigilant and keep mixing! After about 12–15 minutes, the liquid will be at a full boil. Nudge the heat back down to low and keep it at a steady simmer for an additional 15 minutes. Keep stirring slowly and before you know it, the pearls will appear translucent and the surrounding liquid will be quite thick.

Separately, combine the sugar, cornstarch, and salt. Pour in the final ½ cup non-dairy milk to form a loose paste, and mix thoroughly to incorporate all the dry goods. Pour this slurry into the saucepan, stirring again to incorporate. Turn the heat back up to medium and allow the mixture to return to a full boil. Yes, keep stirring all the while—you'll know it's almost done when you genuinely fear that your arm might fall off.

After it comes up to a steady bubble, remove from heat and add the margarine and vanilla, stirring to allow the residual heat to melt the margarine. Gently pour the hot pudding into the prepared crust, trying not to disturb the sliced banana layer at the bottom. Smooth out the top with your spatula and let cool completely. Transfer to the fridge once cool to the touch and chill for at least one hour. Top with a fluffy mound of whipped coconut cream, line the outer edge with sliced bananas, slice and serve!

If you want to prepare the pie in advance, save the banana topping until you plan to serve it, to prevent the slices from shriveling or browning unappealingly. To take out even more browning insurance, quickly toss the slices in a splash of lemon juice, blotting off the excess, before using them to embellish the pie.

BUCKEYE PIE

Makes 8–12 Servings

It took many years and countless batches of peanut butter buckeyes before I ever understood their strange name. Rather than comparing their appearance to eyeballs, they're actually modeled after the buckeye nut. Peanuts are decidedly tastier than buckeyes, and so the swap was made, to the delight of taste buds for centuries to come. Rather than painstakingly rolling dozens of individual spheres before dipping them each into a vat of melted chocolate, save the time and hassle by whipping up this practically instant pie. Cradled in a chocolate crust and blanketed by a ganache topping, the silky peanut butter mousse at the center is far creamier that those simple spheres could ever hope to be.

1 Blind-Baked Chocolate Cookie
   Crust (page 48)
No-Bake Peanut Butter Mousse:
1 12-Ounce Aseptic Package Extra-
   Firm Silken Tofu

1⅓ Cups Creamy Peanut Butter
½ Cup Light Agave Nectar
2 Teaspoons Vanilla Extract
¼ Teaspoon Salt

Chocolate Ganache:
8 Ounces Semi-Sweet Chocolate,
   Finely Chopped (or 1¼ Cups
   Chocolate Chips)
⅔ Cup Plain Non-Dairy Milk

The hardest part of this pie is making the crust, so once it's baked and ready to go, you're more than halfway done!

Lightly drain the tofu of any excess liquid before tossing it into the bowl of your food processor along with all of the remaining ingredients for the peanut butter mousse. Blend until completely pureed, pausing to scrape down the sides of the bowl as needed. When the mousse is homogeneous, perfectly smooth, and lusciously creamy, transfer it into your prepared crust. Smooth out the top with a spatula and set aside.

Combine the chocolate and non-dairy milk in a microwave-safe dish and heat for 60 seconds. Stir thoroughly until the chocolate is fully melted. Continue heating and stirring at intervals of 30 seconds as needed, until silky. Pour the ganache all over the top of the mousse, easing it into all the gaps and edges with your spatula if needed. Tap very gently on the counter a few times to knock out any bubbles.

Chill thoroughly for the ganache to set and yield cleaner slices; at least 3 hours. Okay, so maybe I was wrong—the hardest part will probably be waiting to dive in!

CANNOLI PIE

Makes 8–12
Servings

After a rare outing to our favorite neighborhood pizza place, my sister and I, unstoppable partners in crime during our formative years, would still push our luck for even greater treats. Needling our parents relentlessly, begging to stop at the Italian bakery across the street before returning home, we won the battle of wills more often than not. No matter what else was in the brightly lit pastry case on that day, one of us would always leave with a cannoli in hand, freshly filled to order. Whether it was crowned with pistachios or chocolate chips, or sometimes even sprinkles, the crisp tubes of barely-sweetened ricotta cream could do no wrong. Looking back on it now, I have a feeling my parents were really all too happy to have an excuse to buy themselves a few, too.

1 Blind-Baked Ice Cream Cone Crust
  (page 48) or Vanilla Cookie Crust
  (page 48)
Cashew Mascarpone Filling:
1 Cup Raw Cashews, Soaked for 2
  Hours and Drained
2 Tablespoons Lemon Juice
1 Tablespoon Apple Cider Vinegar

¼ Cup Olive Oil
1 12-Ounce Aseptic Package Extra-
  Firm Silken Tofu, Drained
½ Cup Plain Vegan Yogurt
1 Tablespoon Nutritional Yeast
½ Teaspoon Salt
⅔ Cup Granulated Sugar
1 Tablespoon Cornstarch

1 ½ Teaspoons Agar Powder
To Finish:
2 Tablespoons Mini Chocolate Chips
  or Chocolate Shavings
¼ Cup Roughly Chopped Toasted
  Pistachios

After thoroughly draining away the soaking water from the cashews, toss the nuts into your blender or food processor. Add in the lemon juice, vinegar, and oil, and pulse to incorporate. Once the nuts are broken down, switch to the puree setting and blend thoroughly.

Add the remaining ingredients for the filling, scraping down the sides of the bowl or canister as needed, and blend once more, until completely smooth.

Transfer the creamy mixture to a medium saucepan and set over moderate heat on the stove. Have your prepared crust standing by, because it will move quickly from this point on. Whisk gently but constantly as the filling comes up to temperature, taking care to scrape the bottom and sides of the pan with the whisk to prevent sticking and burning. Wait for bubbles to break steadily on the surface before turning off the heat.

Pour the thick, hot custard into your prepared crust, using a spatula to ease it into all the edges and smooth out the top. Tap the pan on the counter lightly a few times to release any air bubbles that may be trapped within. Let cool to room temperature before moving the pie into your fridge to chill and further set up.

Chill for at least 4 hours before even thinking of cutting into it. Before serving, sprinkle chocolate and chopped pistachios around the outer rim.

CHOCOLATE CHIPOTLE SWEET POTATO PIE

Makes 10–14 Servings

Maybe I've spent a few too many late nights watching food TV, but after one fateful Thanksgiving recipe demo, the sound of chipotle mashed sweet potatoes became too attractive to put out of mind. Presenting such a dish to my straight-up, butter- and cream-mashed potato family would be flat out heresy, so a different approach was clearly needed. Dialing back on the chipotles so that they provided just the slightest tingle on the tongue, their intensity is further tempered by the soothing sweetness of brown sugar and rich coconut milk. Better yet, a thin base of pure dark chocolate adds depth to the dessert. Even those who turn up their noses at traditional sweet potato pie might just change their tune after one bite!

Sure, it may be prepared in an actual pie pan, but with filling this good, I wanted to really pile it on, so the standard equipment simply couldn't accommodate my ideal proportions. Spice levels are completely flexible based on personal preference, so if you're a real chili-head, go ahead and add the full dose, but beware: The difference between ½ of and 1 whole chipotle can be alarming.

1 Blind-Baked Chocolate Cookie
  Crust (page 48) in a 9-Inch
  Round Springform Pan
1 Cup (6 Ounces) Semi-Sweet
  Chocolate Chips

Chipotle Sweet Potato Filling:
2 Cups Roasted Sweet Potato Puree*

1 Cup Dark Brown Sugar, Firmly
  Packed
1 Teaspoon Ground Cinnamon
¼ Teaspoon Ground Nutmeg
¼ Teaspoon Salt
½–1 Small Chipotle Pepper, Canned
  in Adobo Sauce
1 Teaspoon Adobo Sauce

Pinch Freshly Ground Black Pepper
¼ Cup Tapioca Starch
1 Cup Canned Full-Fat Coconut Milk
1 Teaspoon Vanilla Extract

To Finish (Optional):
Coconut Whipped Cream (page 52)
Chocolate Shavings or Curls

*To get roasted sweet potato puree, crank up your oven to 400 degrees. Peel and roughly dice two medium–large sweet potatoes, and toss with about 2 tablespoons of olive oil. Sprinkle very lightly with coarse sea salt, and bake for 20–30 minutes, until the pieces are fork-tender and lightly browned around the edges. Let cool, and puree to a completely smooth consistency in your food processor or blender. Alternately, you could use canned sweet potato or even pumpkin puree.

Preheat your oven to 350 degrees, and bake the chocolate crust as per the instructions, pressed into a lightly greased 9-inch round springform pan. Immediately after removing the crust from the oven, sprinkle it evenly with your chocolate chips, letting them sit for a moment to warm and soften. As they melt, use a spatula to smooth the chocolate out over the crust, to form a fairly even layer. Set aside.

For the filling, simply place all of the ingredients (starting with the lesser amount of chipotle) in your food processor or blender, and pulse to combine. Pause and scrape down the sides of the work bowl as needed, to make sure that everything is getting incorporated, until the filling mixture is completely smooth and homogeneous. Taste for seasoning, and add in more chipotle (or even adobo sauce, if that's not enough for you) as desired. The heat does tone down a bit after being baked, but not too much, so go easy on those spicy little peppers! Once you're satisfied with the level of spice, pour the sweet potato mix on top of your prepared crust, and smooth out the top.

Tap the pan a few times on the counter to release any air bubbles, before sliding it into the oven. Bake for 20–28 minutes, until the edges are set but the center still looks wobbly, much like a cheesecake. Let cool completely before moving the pie into the fridge. Only after it is thoroughly chilled can you top it with the coconut whipped cream and chocolate shavings. Release the ring from the springform pan and serve! And yes, if you added just a touch too much chipotle, a generous scoop of vanilla ice cream does help tame the flame.

DOUBLE CHOCOLATE TRUFFLE TART

Makes 8–12 Servings

Too much is never enough when it comes to chocolate. Why have just one square if there's more to a bar? Who could possibly take just one bite when a second exists? The stuff is simply irresistible in any format, so when translated to a compact slice of tart, it had better pack a serious punch to stand out. Succeeding in that mission with two dark, fudgy layers, this little black dress of the pastry world really is just like an enrobed truffle neatly bundled into a cookie crust. Technically, if you wanted to count the cocoa kick of the shell itself, you could consider this a triple chocolate tart.

1 Unbaked Chocolate Cookie Crust (page 48)

Chocolate Truffle Filling:

9 Ounces Bittersweet Chocolate, Finely Chopped (or 1½ Cups Chocolate Chips)

¼ Cup Non-Dairy Margarine or Coconut Oil

1 Ripe Medium-Sized Avocado

⅓ Cup Plain Vegan Creamer or Canned Full-Fat Coconut Milk

⅓ Cup Granulated Sugar

¼ Teaspoon Salt

1 Teaspoon Vanilla Extract

Chocolate Fudge Glaze:

1½ Teaspoons Agar Powder

½ Cup Granulated Sugar

⅔ Cup Dutch-Processed Cocoa Powder, Sifted

⅓ Cup Water

2 Tablespoons Light Corn Syrup or Agave Nectar

¼ Cup Plain Vegan Creamer or Canned Full-Fat Coconut Milk

Preheat your oven to 350 degrees.

Starting with the truffle filling, place both the chocolate and margarine or coconut oil in a microwave-safe bowl and heat on full power for 60 seconds. Stir thoroughly, and if not fully melted, continue heating and stirring at intervals of 30 seconds, until the chocolate is completely smooth. Be careful not to burn the chocolate; it will ultimately take much more stirring than heating. Set aside for the time being.

Pull out your food processor or blender, and toss the avocado, creamer, sugar, salt, and vanilla into the work bowl. Puree until smooth, pausing to scrape down the sides to reincorporate errant pieces of avocado as needed. Once the mixture is entirely lump-free, pour in all of the melted chocolate and pulse to incorporate. Blend just until the mixture is homogeneous; you don't want to whip too much air into the mixture, since it should be a dense and decadent fudge once set.

Transfer the truffle filling to your prepared pie crust, smoothing it out evenly across the bottom. Tap the pan on the counter a few times to release any trapped air bubbles before moving the pie into the oven. Bake for 20–25 minutes, until slightly puffed in the center and set around the edges. The center should still jiggle slightly when the pan is gently tapped, as it will continue to firm up as it cools. Let cool for at least 30 minutes before glazing.

While the pie cools, go ahead and prepare the glaze. Place the agar, sugar, and cocoa in a medium saucepan, and whisk thoroughly to distribute all of the dry ingredients throughout the mixture. Slowly pour in the water, starting with just a few tablespoons, and stir it into a thick paste. Once there are no lumps or dry patches remaining, pour in the remaining water, along with the syrup and creamer. Turn on the heat to medium and whisk gently. Be careful not to go crazy and beat bubbles into the glaze, as you want this to be unblemished when it solidifies on the top of the pie.

When the mixture just begins to boil, turn off the heat, and carefully pour the glaze over the baked filling. Use your spatula to gently spread it across the entire surface in an even layer. Finally, move the pie into the fridge and let chill for at least three hours before slicing and indulging.

FIGGY PUDDING PIE

Makes 8–12 Servings

What the British call "pudding" is what I'd consider a more edible version of fruitcake, but I'm more than happy to slap any old name on it so long as I can steal a bite. No winter season would be complete without some rendition of a figgy pudding, as the classic Christmas carol can attest. Obviously, figs tend to be the featured fruit, but I've sneakily swapped in prunes and dates before with great results, too.

1 Unbaked Classic Crust (Page 36)

Figgy Pudding:

¼ Cup Non-Dairy Margarine

½ Cup Dark Brown Sugar, Firmly Packed

½ Teaspoon Salt

1 Teaspoon Ground Cinnamon

½ Teaspoon Ground Nutmeg

¼ Teaspoon Ground Cloves

¼ Teaspoon Ground Allspice

¼ Teaspoon Baking Soda

¼ Teaspoon Baking Powder

¼ Cup Unsweetened Applesauce

½ Cup Molasses

¾ Pound Dried Black Mission Figs, Chopped Small (About 2 Cups Lightly Packed)

⅓ Cup Plain Non-Dairy Milk

1 Tablespoon Lemon Juice

½ Teaspoon Orange Zest

½ Cup Unseasoned Bread Crumbs

⅓ Cup All-Purpose Flour

To Finish:

¼ Cup Brandy, Bourbon, or Rum

Vanilla Hard Sauce (Optional):

1 Cup Plain Non-Dairy Milk

½ Cup Granulated Sugar

1½ Tablespoons Cornstarch

2 Tablespoons Non-Dairy Margarine

⅛ Teaspoon Salt

1 Teaspoon Vanilla Extract

2 Tablespoons Rum

Preheat your oven to 325 degrees.

In the bowl of your stand mixer, beat the margarine to soften slightly before adding in the brown sugar. Cream together thoroughly, until fluffy and homogeneous. Scrape down the sides of the bowl with your spatula to ensure that everything gets mixed together, and sprinkle in the salt, all of the spices, baking powder, and baking soda next. Mix briefly to incorporate.

In a separate bowl, stir together the applesauce, molasses, chopped dried figs, non-dairy milk, lemon juice, and orange zest. Add about half of the flour and bread crumbs into the stand mixer first, stirring lightly, before pouring in half of the liquid ingredient mixture. Once mostly mixed in, follow that up with the remainder of the dry, and then the rest of the wet goods. Mix gently until mostly smooth; a few lumps are just fine.

Transfer the batter to your waiting pie crust, distributing the chunks of fig as evenly as possible throughout. Tap the whole pan on the counter lightly to knock out any air bubbles, and smooth out the top with your spatula.

Continued on page 84.

Tent the pie with aluminum foil and bake for 40 minutes. At that point, remove the foil and bake for a final 25–30 minutes longer, until golden brown on top and a toothpick inserted into the center pulls out with just a few moist crumbs sticking to it. While still warm, brush evenly with your alcoholic beverage of choice, so that the booze can soak in and fully absorb. Let cool for at least 20 minutes before enjoying with a drizzle of hard sauce, if desired. This pie is best served warm, but is also delightful at room temperature. Like many alcohol-soaked cakes, this pie tastes even better the next day.

To make the hard sauce, whisk together the non-dairy milk, sugar, cornstarch, and salt in a medium saucepan. Be sure to beat out any clumps of starch before turning on the heat to medium. Bring the mixture to a boil, whisking constantly so that it remains smooth. Add in the margarine, stirring until melted and fully incorporated, and then turn off the heat. Whisk in the vanilla and rum last, and let cool before serving. It will continue to thicken as it cools, so if you plan to prepare it in advance or serve it chilled, you may want to stir in a splash more non-dairy milk or rum to achieve your desired consistency.

COOKIES 'N CREME FRIED PIES

Makes 8–10 Servings

On one fateful day at a state fair not too long ago, one daring soul that toed the line between brilliance and insanity threw caution to the wind—and battered Oreos® into the deep fryer. The decadent treat took off like wildfire, and what was once a bizarre novelty can now be found on menus across the country. Really, Oreos were already "America's favorite cookie," so it's hard to go too far wrong by dressing them up a bit. Taking it one step further as I can't help but do, my interpretation wraps up a bit of custard filling with big chunks of chocolate sandwich cookies in personal pocket pies. Consider it merely the next step among many in the evolution of this once humble pantry staple.

1 Unbaked and Unrolled Classic
Crust (page 36)
Cookies 'n Creme Custard:
1¼ Cups Plain Vegan Creamer
½ Teaspoon Agar Powder

¼ Cup Granulated Sugar
2 Tablespoons Cornstarch
Pinch Salt
½ Teaspoon Vanilla Extract

8 Quartered Chocolate Sandwich
Cookies (About 1 Heaping Cup)
To Finish:
Oil for Frying

In a medium saucepan, vigorously whisk together the creamer, agar, sugar, cornstarch, and salt. Be sure to beat out any lumps or remaining pockets of dry ingredients before turning on the heat to medium. Cook, whisking periodically, until the mixture comes to a full boil. Reduce the heat slightly to keep the liquid at a simmer, stirring while it slowly bubbles for an additional two minutes.

Turn off the stove and let the hot custard cool to room temperature, about 30–60 minutes. Do not refrigerate it, or it will set up too firmly. As it is, the pudding should thicken considerably after it stands. Beat briefly with the whisk to smooth it out once more. Fold in the quartered cookies with a spatula and set aside.

At this point, you can begin preheating your oil in a high-sided skillet or deep stock pot. Pour in enough oil to reach ¾ inch in depth, and use a deep-frying or candy thermometer to know when the oil hits 375 degrees.

Meanwhile, for the crusts, roll out your prepared and chilled dough on a lightly floured surface. As per usual, aim for an even ⅛ inch in thickness. Using round cookie cutters that measure between 4 ½–5 inches in diameter, punch out as many circles of dough as your crust will allow. Gather any scraps, re-roll, and repeat as needed, until the dough is used up.

Continued on page 87.

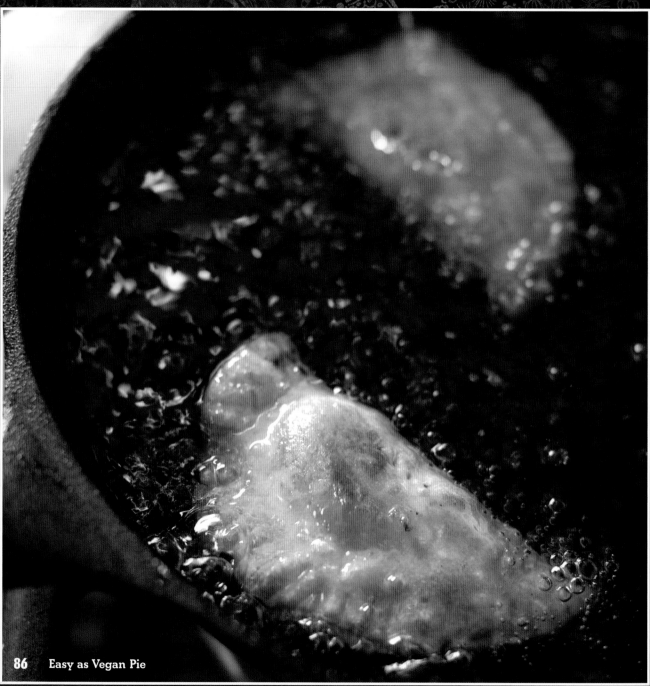

Spoon 1–2 tablespoons of filling into the center of each circle. Resist the temptation to over-stuff them, or else they'll burst and empty out while frying. Use lightly moistened fingers to trace the inner rim of the circles to act as "glue", folding them in half and pressing down gently but firmly around the half-moons. Use a fork dipped in flour to go back over the edge and crimp the pies. Take a very sharp knife to the tops and cut 2 or 3 small slits to vent the steam.

Carefully ease only 2 or 3 pies into the hot oil at a time. The last thing you want to do is crowd them, which will suddenly lower the temperature and cause the pastry to soak up far more grease. Cook for 3–5 minutes per side, flipping gently with a slotted spatula or wire spider. Transfer to an overturned cooling rack set on paper towels, and let cool for at least 10 minutes before enjoying so that you don't burn your mouth! Repeat the frying process for the remaining pies.

Fear of frying? That's okay, these can be baked, too. Prepare the pie pockets as previously instructed, but place them about 1 inch apart on silpat- or parchment-lined baking sheets. Brush the tops liberally with oil, and bake at 375 degrees for 15–20 minutes. Flip after about 10 minutes and bake until golden brown.

GREEK SILK PIE

**Makes 8–10
Servings**

After a hectic day, a simple yet satisfying dessert is order. Chocolate pie, ready in a flash and healthy enough to justify one generous wedge per person, fits the bill perfectly. Inspired by the wholly decadent butter- and egg-laden French silk pie, this is a less sweet, less unctuous, and far less guilt-inducing version that you could possibly get away with eating for breakfast. At least I hope so, because that's what I did.

1 Blind-Baked Classic Crust (page
  36) or Chocolate Pastry Crust
  (pages 36-37)
3 Ounces Unsweetened (100%
  Cacao) Chocolate

½ Cup Non-Dairy Margarine
¾ Cup Granulated Sugar
3 Tablespoons Dutch-Processed
  Cocoa Powder
Pinch Salt

1 Teaspoon Instant Coffee Powder
1 Teaspoon Vanilla Extract
2 6-Ounce Containers Greek-Style
  Vanilla Coconut or Almond
  Yogurt, Divided

Begin by melting down the chocolate either in a double-boiler or in the microwave, heating at intervals of 30 seconds and stirring well until smooth. Set aside and let cool for at least 15 minutes.

In the bowl of your stand mixer, thoroughly cream together the margarine and sugar as if you were making cookies, until light and fluffy. Beat in the cocoa, salt, coffee powder, and vanilla, followed by one of the containers of Greek "yogurt." Scrape down the sides of the bowl with a spatula, and mix well. Don't worry if the mixture looks grainy at this point.

Add in the melted chocolate, and whip on high for 3 minutes. Slowly incorporate the final container of "yogurt," and then resume beating the filling on high speed for an additional 2–3 minutes, until smooth.

Pour the filling into your prepared pie crust, tap it lightly on the counter to release any air bubbles that may be trapped within, and smooth down the top evenly. Refrigerate for at least 3 hours before serving.

Top slices with a generous dollop of vegan whipped cream, if desired.

KIWI COCONUT PIE

Makes 8-10
Servings

Tangy kiwi fruits brighten up any salad or snack, and that punchy flavor makes them the perfect counterpoint to creamy coconut custard. Cutting the richness while complimenting the tropical vibe, these slices have the edge on plain any old coconut pie.

1 Unbaked Classic Crust (page 36)
Kiwi-Coconut Custard:
6 Ounces (½ Aseptic Package) Extra-
   Firm Silken Tofu
1 Cup Canned Full-Fat Coconut Milk
1 Cup Granulated Sugar

3 Tablespoons Non-Dairy Margarine,
   Melted
2 Tablespoons All-Purpose Flour
1 Teaspoon Vanilla Extract
1¼ Cups Unsweetened Shredded
   Coconut
3 Medium Kiwis

1 ½ Tablespoons Cornstarch

To Finish:
¼ Cup Unsweetened Coconut Shreds
   or Flakes, Toasted
2 Medium Kiwis

Preheat your oven to 350 degrees.

Using a food processor or blender, purée the tofu until completely smooth. Add in the coconut milk and sugar, pulsing to combine. Melt the margarine, then mix it in, along with the flour and vanilla. Fold in the shredded coconut by hand.

Peel and chop the kiwis, discarding the fuzzy skin. In a separate bowl, toss them with the cornstarch to fully coat all of the pieces of fruit. Gently stir them into the coconut custard and pour the resulting mixture into your unbaked crust.

Bake for 45 to 55 minutes, until the crust is nicely browned and the filling appears to have risen a bit. The pie will still be wobbly in the center, but it will continue to set up as it cools. Let the pie sit for at least an hour before sprinkling the toasted coconut on top and garnishing with the remaining two kiwis, peeled and sliced as desired. If you want to add a bit of whimsy to your presentation, use small cookie cutters to punch fun shapes out of individual fruit slices. Serve, and watch the smiles spread!

LEMON CHIA SEED MERINGUE PIE

Makes 8–10 Servings

When I initially broke the news that my next cookbook venture would be focused on pies, after the congratulations were dispensed, the first question would invariably be some permutation of: "Will there be a lemon meringue pie?" A favorite pie for many but one that's been notably absent from most vegan repertoires, I don't blame them. The bane of many eggless bakers, a fluffy meringue topping has been just beyond reach . . . until now. Crowning an assertively citrus curd flecked with chia seeds, it's my updated take on the classic lemon poppy seed pairing.

1 Blind-Baked Classic Crust (page 36)
Lemon-Chia Seed Curd:
1 ½ Cups Water
1 Tablespoon Whole Chia Seeds
Zest of 2 Small or 1 Large Lemon
¾ Cup Fresh Lemon Juice

1¼ Cups Granulated Sugar
¼ Cup Arrowroot
1 Tablespoon Agar Powder
¼ Teaspoon Ground Turmeric
  (Optional, for Color)
⅛ Teaspoon Salt

2 Tablespoons Non-Dairy Margarine
  or Coconut Oil

To Finish:
½ Batch Meringue (page 54)

After baking your pie shell, go ahead and turn off the oven since the rest of this pie is made on the stove.

Whisk together the water, chia seeds, lemon zest, and lemon juice, then let the mixture stand for 15 minutes. This will let the chia seeds begin to gel.

In a medium saucepan, combine the sugar, arrowroot, agar, turmeric, and salt, stirring to distribute the ingredients evenly throughout the mixture. Once the seeds have formed a gel, pour the seeds and remaining liquids into the saucepan, whisking vigorously to incorporate. Make sure that the agar and starch are dissolved in the mixture before turning on the heat to medium. Cook, stirring occasionally, until the mixture comes to a full boil. Drop in the margarine or coconut oil and cook for 1–2 minutes longer, whisking all the while, until melted and seamlessly blended in.

Turn off the heat and let the hot, loose curd sit for about 10 minutes, whisking frequently, allowing it to cool down a bit. This will help it thicken before it hits the prepared pie shell, ensuring that the seeds stay suspended throughout, rather than floating to the top. While it's still very liquid in consistency, pour the curd into your baked crust, and let it cool to room temperature before moving it.

Transfer to the fridge for 2–3 hours, to chill and fully set.

When ready to serve, whip up the meringue according to the recipe's instructions and apply it to the pie, either in big dollops or piped puffs. Place the pie on the top rack of your oven with the broiler set to high, rotating the pie every minute or two for even browning. Once all the tips of the meringue are golden, quickly remove the pie and serve right away.

MUD PIE

Makes 10–12 Servings

Go ahead and play in the mud! Inspired by the call for a "cup of mud," which is of course simply coffee, and the outrageously chocolaty affair known as Mississippi mud cake, it's as dark and intense as a fresh brewed cuppa, but with all the trappings of an elegant dessert. Don't be misled by the funky name—this kind of mud pie is far tastier than any childhood sandbox creation.

1 Blind-Baked Chocolate Cookie
   Crust (page 48)

Mocha Mousse:
12 Ounces (2 Cups) Semi-Sweet
   Chocolate Chips
2 Tablespoons Light Agave Nectar
¼ Cup Plain Non-Dairy Milk

3 Ripe, Medium-Sized Avocados
2 Tablespoons Instant Coffee Powder
½ Teaspoon Salt

Ganache Drizzle:
⅓ Cup (2 Ounces) Semi-Sweet
   Chocolate Chips
2 Tablespoons Plain Non-Dairy Milk

To Finish:
¾ Cup Dark Chocolate-Covered
   Espresso Beans, Roughly
   Chopped

Perfect for a pie novice, this is another effortless dessert with a big flavor payoff. Once your crust is baked and cooled, all you have to do is combine the chocolate, agave, and "milk" in a microwave-safe container. Start by heating for 60 seconds, stirring vigorously to help the chips melt. Heat for additional 30-second intervals, stirring well after each, until the mixture is entirely lump-free.

Transfer the melted chocolate into the bowl of your food processor or blender, along with the pitted and peeled avocados. Add the coffee powder and salt, and let it rip! Blend until pureed to a flawless, silky-smooth consistency, pausing periodically to scrape any unincorporated avocado off the sides of the bowl. Pour the thick mousse into your prepared crust, smooth out the top with a spatula, and chill for a minimum of 2–3 hours, to allow the filling to set.

For the ganache, simply melt together the chocolate and "milk" using the same method as before. Drizzle all over the top of the pie, and don't hold back—let your inner Jackson Pollock out and make it a chocolate work of art! Finish by sprinkling chopped chocolate-covered espresso beans around the rim. Take a moment to admire your masterpiece before it's devoured.

NEW YORK CHEESECAKE PIE

*Makes 10–12
Servings*

Nebulous and highly contested in definition, the only thing that most can agree on about New York-style cheesecake is that it must smack of cream cheese tang, slice smoothly, and have a density comparable to lead. Fruit toppings are also hotly debated, and while cherry strikes me as the most "authentic," feel free to throw caution to the wind and swirl in any sort of jam you fancy. Though real New Yorkers might not agree on most topics, at the end of the day, I think that anyone who eats this no-fuss rendition would happily enjoy it without further debate.

1 Unbaked Graham Cracker Crust
   (page 48) or Vanilla Cookie Crust
   (page 48)
Cheesecake Filling:
1 8-Ounce Package Vegan Cream
   Cheese

1 Cup Vegan Sour Cream or Plain
   Vegan Greek-Style Yogurt
½ Cup Granulated Sugar
3 Tablespoons Cornstarch
1 Tablespoon Lemon Juice
1½ Teaspoons Vanilla Extract
¼ Teaspoon Salt

To Finish:
½ Cup Cherry Preserves or Jam
Coconut Whipped Cream (page 52)
   (Optional)
Maraschino Cherries (Optional)

Preheat your oven to 325 degrees.

For the filling, pull out your stand mixer and toss in all of the ingredients except for the preserves. Using the paddle attachment, beat thoroughly, scraping down the sides of the bowl as needed to incorporate everything, until completely smooth. Pour the filling into the prepared, unbaked crust, tapping the pan gently on the counter to remove any air bubbles.

If your preserves or jam is particularly thick, microwave briefly for just 10–20 seconds to loosen it up. It should be just a hair thinner than spreadable consistency. If need be, stir in a teaspoon of water. Drizzle the fruit spread all around the top of the cheesecake and then take a wooden skewer or chopstick to further swirl it in.

Bake for 45–50 minutes, until the sides begin to pull away from the pan but the center still appears slightly wobbly when tapped.

Let cool to room temperature before stashing in the fridge for at least 3 hours until thoroughly chilled. Top slices with dainty tufts of whipped coconut cream and maraschino cherries if desired.

NUTTERSCOTCH PIE

*Makes 8–12
Servings*

Salted caramel has been going through a renaissance lately, but the other amber-hued elixir known as butterscotch can be brightened in just the same way with a modest saline addition. At the intersection of brown sugar and creamy almond butter, the flavors really come to life with hints of vanilla, real scotch, and of course a bit of salt to seal the deal.

1 Blind-Baked Classic Crust
   (page 36)

Almond-Butterscotch Pudding:
¼ Cup Non-Dairy Margarine
1 Cup Dark Brown Sugar, Firmly
   Packed

¾ Teaspoon Salt
¼ Cup Cornstarch
2½ Cups Plain Non-Dairy Milk
½ Cup Creamy Almond Butter
1 Tablespoon Scotch or Bourbon
   (Optional)
1 Teaspoon Vanilla Extract

To Finish:
1 Batch Whipped Coconut Cream
   (page 52)
Toasted Sliced Almonds (Optional)

In a medium saucepan, melt the margarine over low heat. Add the brown sugar and whisk until the brown sugar dissolves and begins to bubble all over.

Meanwhile, whisk together the salt, cornstarch, and non-dairy milk in a separate bowl, stirring vigorously to break up any stubborn lumps of starch that may form. Once the sugar is starting to sizzle, slowly pour the "milk" mixture into the pan, standing back slightly to protect yourself from any potential splatters. Whisk thoroughly to incorporate.

Allow the mixture to cook, stirring every minute or so, until it bubbles slowly around the edges and begins to thicken. Add in the almond butter, beating with the whisk to disperse it smoothly throughout the custard. Whisk constantly from this point on, scraping the sides and bottom of the pan repeatedly to prevent scorching. Allow it to come up to a full boil, and then immediately turn off the heat. Finally, stir in the scotch or bourbon, if using, along with the vanilla.

Pour the hot butterscotch pudding into your prepared pie shell and let cool to room temperature. Chill for at least three hours, or overnight to yield the cleanest slices.

Right before serving, smooth dollops of whipped coconut cream over the entire exposed surface, swirling decoratively as desired. For an extra flourish, go all out and sprinkle slices with almonds.

PISTACHIO PUDDING PIE

*Makes 8–12
Servings*

Look up a recipe, any recipe, for pistachio pie, and 9 times out of 10 you'll end up with instructions that call for a box of instant pudding mix. The lack of real pistachios is only the start of this abject culinary failure, followed closely by the inclusion of synthetic coloring and a veritable bucket of sugar. That's where it ends if you're lucky, but don't forget about all the tasty preservatives that could be lurking in just one little box. Skip the mix and opt in for real flavor. This pudding pie doesn't skimp on the pistachios, and adds a more natural shade of green with a handful of spinach. It's not quite instant, but every minute of work is more than worth the effort.

1 Blind-Baked Graham Cracker Crust
    (page 48) or Vanilla Cookie Crust
    (page 48)

Pistachio Pudding:
1½ Cups Toasted, Shelled Pistachios
⅔ Cup Granulated Sugar

½ Cup Fresh Baby Spinach, Lightly
    Packed (Optional, for Color)
1 Medium-Sized, Ripe Avocado
1 Teaspoon Lemon Juice
2 Cups Plain Non-Dairy Milk
3½ Tablespoons Cornstarch
⅛ Teaspoon Salt

¼ Teaspoon Ground Ginger
1½ Teaspoons Vanilla Extract

To Finish:
Whipped Coconut Cream (page 52)
¼ Cup Roughly Chopped, Toasted
    Pistachios

To get things started, toss the nuts and sugar into your food processor and grind them down into a thick, doughy sort of paste. This can take as long as 10 minutes, so be patient and don't rush this step. After about 5 minutes, pause to scrape down the sides of the work bowl and add in the spinach, if using. It may take some coaxing to incorporate and break down, so be prepared to stop and ease the leaves back towards the blade, as needed. Once the pistachios have begun to surrender their natural oils and are pretty well pulverized, stop the machine, and add in the pitted and peeled avocado, along with the lemon juice.

The mixture will become very thick at this point. Begin slowly drizzling in the non-dairy milk, but add just enough to allow the contents of the container to puree easily; about half of the total measure. Once the mixture is perfectly smooth, pour in the remainder of the non-dairy milk, and incorporate the cornstarch, salt, and ginger as well. Pulse to combine.

When completely pureed, transfer the green liquid to a medium saucepan set over medium heat. Cook, stirring constantly and scraping the bottom and sides of the pan to prevent burning, until thickened in consistency and bubbles begin to break on the surface. Turn off the stove, stir in the vanilla, and transfer to your prepared crust.

Spread the custard out evenly within the pan and smooth out the top with your spatula. Let cool at room temperature for about 15 minutes before stashing the pie in your fridge. Chill for at least 3–4 hours before even thinking of slicing into it.

Right before serving, pipe whipped coconut cream around the entire border and sprinkle the chopped pistachios on top.

RASPBERRY RED VELVET PIE

Serves 8-10

I must admit, the charms of traditional red velvet are lost on me. If not for the cream cheese frosting on top, I'm not sure I would have ever been swayed to take a bite in the first place. Not a bad cake by any means, it just strikes me as a bit lacking in the flavor department. Subtlety is not my strong suit, so I can't help but crave a bolder taste than the traditional mild cocoa and vanilla essence. However, mix in some crimson red berries to amp up the flavor and hue all in one fell swoop, and now we're talking. Above all else though, don't even dream of leaving off that cream cheese frosting!

1 Blind-Baked Vanilla Cookie Crust
　　(page 48) or Graham Cracker
　　Crust (page 48)

Raspberry Red Velvet Pudding:
12 Ounces Frozen Raspberries,
　　Thawed (About 1½ Cups)
1 Small Red Beet (About 2.5
　　Ounces), Cooked and Peeled*

¾ Cup Granulated Sugar
3 Tablespoons Natural Cocoa Powder
1 Tablespoon Lemon Juice
⅛ Teaspoon Salt
1 Cup Water
1¾ Teaspoons Agar Powder
1 Teaspoon Vanilla Extract

Cream Cheese Frosting:
½ Cup (4 Ounces) Vegan Cream
　　Cheese
¼ Cup Non-Dairy Margarine
4-5 Cups Confectioner's Sugar
½ Teaspoon Vanilla Extract

Place the thawed berries into your food processor, and chop the beet roughly before adding it in as well. Pulse until blended, and then incorporate the sugar, cocoa powder, lemon juice, and salt. Thoroughly puree, for about 5 minutes, to ensure that the raspberries are as broken down as possible. It will still be rough-looking due to the seeds, but there should be no chunks of beet remaining.

Strain the mixture through a fine mesh sieve into a medium saucepan, discarding the raspberry seeds. Vigorously whisk the agar powder into the water before adding both into the saucepan. Whisk the whole mixture to combine. Cook over medium heat, stirring periodically and scraping the bottom to ensure that nothing sticks, until bubbles begin to break at a steady rate on the surface. From that point, simmer for an additional two minutes before turning off the heat and mixing in the vanilla. Gently pour the hot, liquefied filling into your prepared crust.

Let cool, undisturbed, until it reaches room temperature. It should be much firmer at that point, so you can easily transfer it to the fridge to chill.

For the frosting, place both the cream cheese and margarine in the bowl of your stand mixer and cream together thoroughly. Once smooth, add the confectioner's sugar and vanilla, and begin mixing again on a low speed. Pause to

Continued on page 104.

scrape down the sides of the bowl, and then gradually increase the speed to high. Whip for 4–5 minutes, until light and fluffy.

Once the pie is thoroughly chilled, either pipe the frosting decoratively around the border, or spoon dollops onto individual slices. Garnish with fresh raspberries right before serving.

*Unlike many root vegetables, beets are much easier to cook with the skin on. Once tender all the way through, that peel will slip right off, which is also a good indication of when it's properly done. Place your beet in a large square of aluminum foil, and wrap it so that it's completely enclosed. Toss the foil package into an oven preheated to 400 degrees, and roast for 45–60 minutes, depending on the size of the beet. Let cool until you can handle it without burning yourself, and rub the exterior until the skin comes off. You may need to take a peeler to any stubborn spots.

ROCK 'N ROLL ELVIS PIE

Makes 10–14 Servings

The King of Rock and Roll was infamous for his legendary food cravings, the peanut butter, banana, and bacon sandwich especially. Clearly the man was a gastronome ahead of his time, combining sweet, salty, and savory well before anyone knew what umami or flavor pairing was. It sounds crazy on paper, but give it the benefit of the doubt and just try a bite; for reasons not fully known, it just works.

1 Unbaked Vanilla Cookie Crust (page 48) or Graham Cracker Crust (page 48)

Banana Layer:

2 Medium-Size Ripe Bananas, Cut into ¼-Inch Slices

½ Teaspoon Lemon Juice

Peanut Butter Crème:

¾ Cup Creamy Peanut Butter

1 12-Ounce Aseptic Package Extra-Firm Silken Tofu

1 Cup Confectioner's Sugar

½ Teaspoon Vanilla Extract

¼ Teaspoon Salt

Oinkless Bacon Peanut Brittle:

1 Cup Granulated Sugar

½ Cup Light Corn Syrup or Light Agave Nectar

¼ Cup Water

1 Teaspoon Vanilla Extract

1 Teaspoon Baking Soda

½ Cup Roasted, Salted Peanuts

½ Cup Coconut Bacon (page 57)

The brittle will need ample time to cool, so that's a good place to start when creating this pie. Set out a silpat on a baking sheet near the stove.

In a medium saucepan with high sides, combine the sugar, corn syrup or agave, and water over medium heat. Stir until the sugar dissolves, and then keep your spatula out of the pan to prevent crystals from forming. After the syrup comes to a boil, attach a candy thermometer to the side of the pan, and cook without stirring until the mixture reaches 290–300 degrees, or right between the soft and hard crack stage.

Immediately remove from the heat and stir in the vanilla, baking soda, peanuts, and bacon. Be cautious, as the mixture will bubble and sputter angrily. Very quickly pour the hot mixture onto your prepared baking sheet, using your spatula to distribute the goodies more evenly if necessary. Do not flatten the mixture, as you want those little air bubbles intact.

Cool for at least 15–20 minutes before breaking into raisin-sized pieces. Set aside or store in an airtight container at room temperature for 5–7 days.

Continued on page 107.

As for the pie itself, first toss the banana slices with the lemon juice to prevent them from browning. Arrange them in an even layer at the bottom of your prepared crust, overlapping as needed to completely cover the entire surface. Stash the pie in the fridge while moving on to the crème filling.

Pull out your food processor or blender, and place all of the ingredients for the peanut butter crème inside. Pulse first to incorporate, and then turn it up to puree. Pause to scrape down the sides of the work bowl with your spatula, to ensure that there are no remaining chunks of tofu, and blend once more. When the mixture is completely smooth, retrieve your banana-lined crust and pour the crème on top. Smooth the filling with your spatula, and move the whole pie back into the fridge. Chill for at least 4–6 hours before slicing, and overnight to ensure the cleanest cuts.

Right before serving, sprinkle liberally with the chopped bacon brittle.

SKINNY MINT TART

Makes 8–10 Servings

Once a member of the Girl Scout gang, I too terrorized my neighbors with annual threats of boxes upon boxes of cookies. The phase didn't last long, but my love for those simple chocolate-covered Thin Mints® sure did. Mint and chocolate are simply a match made in heaven, in any format, so it was easy to imagine a refreshing herbal kick every time I snacked on scraps of chocolate cookie crust. For an extra minty burst, try adding a splash of peppermint extract into the crust and/or ganache, too.

1 Unbaked Chocolate Cookie Crust (page 48), in a 13¾- x 4½-inch Rectangular Tart Pan or 9-inch Round Tart Pan with Removable Bottom

Peppermint Crème:

2 Ripe Medium-Size Avocados, Peeled and Pitted

1½ Teaspoons Lemon Juice
1¼ Teaspoons Peppermint Extract
½ Teaspoon Vanilla Extract
¾ Cup Plain Non-Dairy Milk
1 Cup Granulated Sugar
3 Tablespoons Cornstarch
Pinch Salt

Ganache:

6 Ounces (1 Cup) Semi-Sweet Chocolate Chips
¼ Cup Plain Non-Dairy Milk
1 Tablespoon Non-Dairy Margarine or Coconut Oil

No need to heat up the kitchen with the oven, as this little number is a no-bake treat. Instead, grab your blender or food processor, and place the avocados, lemon juice, peppermint and vanilla extract inside. Blend until thoroughly pureed, pausing to scrape down the sides of the canister as needed. Once smooth, set aside.

Place a medium saucepan over moderate heat, and vigorously whisk together the non-dairy milk, sugar, cornstarch, and salt. Be sure to beat out any potential lumps of starch before things really start cooking. Stir occasionally until the mixture comes to a full, rolling boil, and turn off the heat. Quickly pour the hot custard into your blender full of avocado, and pulse to incorporate. Give it one last blitz to ensure that the mixture is perfectly homogeneous, and pour the crème filling into your prepared crust. Let cool to room temperature before stashing the tart in your fridge.

For the ganache, combine the chocolate, non-dairy milk, and margarine or coconut oil in a microwave-safe container. Heat for 60 seconds. Stir thoroughly, even if it doesn't look completely melted–it should come together after a bit of agitation, but if the chocolate still isn't entirely smooth, return to the microwave for 15-30 seconds at a time, watching carefully to ensure that it doesn't burn. Drizzle ganache over the top of the tart as artfully or wildly as you please. Allow at least 4 hours for the tart to chill and firm up before serving.

SPECULOOS PUMPKIN PIE

Already enriched with all the spices of the season, a creamy smear of speculoos spread is an effortless way to liven up the classic pie. Serving as both a flavoring agent and binder, the rich texture is unlike any other rendition I've sampled, before or after going vegan. Not everyone in my family is a pumpkin lover, but come Thanksgiving, everyone is more than happy to dig into this particular pie.

1 Unbaked Classic Crust (page 36) or
   Wholesome Whole Wheat Crust
   (page 44)

Speculoos-Pumpkin Custard:
1 15-Ounce Can (1¾ Cups)
   Pumpkin Puree
⅔ Cup Speculoos Spread (page 63)
½ Cup Granulated Sugar

¼ Cup Dark Brown Sugar, Firmly
   Packed
1 Tablespoon Arrowroot
1 Tablespoon Cornstarch
1 Teaspoon Ground Cinnamon
½ Teaspoon Ground Nutmeg
½ Teaspoon Ground Ginger
½ Teaspoon Salt

½ Teaspoon Vanilla Extract
1 Cup Plain Non-Dairy Milk

To Finish (Optional):
Whipped Coconut Cream (page 52)
Speculoos Cookies (page 60)

Preheat your oven to 350 degrees.

In a large bowl or the bowl of your stand mixer, beat together the pumpkin puree, speculoos spread, and both sugars. Mix until smooth and homogeneous, then add in the cornstarch, all of the spices, salt, and vanilla. Once incorporated, slowly drizzle in the non-dairy milk while continuing to stir. Scrape down the sides of the bowl thoroughly to ensure that the whole mixture is completely smooth before proceeding.

Pour the filling into your crust-lined pie pan and gently slide the whole thing into the oven.

Bake for 20 minutes, undisturbed. Without opening the oven door, reduce the temperature to 325 degrees. Bake another 30–40 minutes or until a toothpick inserted into the center of the pie comes out clean. Cool for at least 2 hours and serve at room temperature.

For an extra-fancy presentation, garnish with dollops of whipped coconut cream and whole speculoos cookies.

WATERMELON CHIFFON PIE

Makes 8–12 Servings

Aside from the typical fruit salad or icy granita, how many watermelon desserts are there? Not many, and even fewer that are actually worth eating. Break the mold with a truly unique watermelon treat. A curious juxtaposition of refreshing fruit against a creamy, fluffy backdrop, each slice is a little taste of summer in a crust.

1 Blind-Baked Vanilla Cookie Crust
   (page 48)

Watermelon Chiffon:
2½ Cups Watermelon Juice (From
   About 6 Cups Diced Watermelon)

¼ Cup Water
¼–⅓ Cup Granulated Sugar,
   Depending on the Sweetness of
   the Melon
1 Tablespoon Lemon Juice
2 Teaspoons Agar Powder

¼ Teaspoon Xanthan Gum
1 14-Ounce Can Full-Fat Coconut
   Milk, Chilled for at Least 2 Hours

To Serve (Optional):
Whipped Coconut Cream (page 52)

Making watermelon juice is much simpler than it may sound, and definitely doesn't require any fancy equipment. Just toss the diced watermelon flesh into your blender, and let it rip on high speed. Blend thoroughly, for about 2–3 minutes, until the melon is entirely liquefied. Pass the juice through a fine mesh sieve and discard the solids. Voila, you have your juice ready to go!

Measure out 2½ cups of juice and transfer it back into your blender. Add the water, sugar, and lemon juice, and pulse to combine. Allow the motor to run continuously while slowly sprinkling in the agar and xanthan gum, aiming for the center of the vortex that forms in the liquid. If the xanthan were mixed in without the constant agitation, it would immediately clump and turn slimy, so make sure it's not just sticking to the walls of the blender.

Pour the juice mixture into a medium saucepan and set it over medium heat on the stove. Whisk periodically until it comes to a boil. Turn off the heat and cool for about 10–15 minutes.

Meanwhile, open the can of chilled coconut milk without shaking it and skim off the thick top layer of coconut cream. Discard or save the remaining coconut water for another use.

Place the coconut cream in the bowl of your stand mixer with the whisk attachment installed. Begin beating on low speed. Gradually increase until you reach the highest speed setting, and continue whipping for about 5 minutes, until the mixture is light and fluffy.

At this point, the melon juice mixture should have thickened quite a bit. Stir in half of the whipped coconut cream with a wide spatula, until homogeneous. Fold in the second half of the whipped cream much more gently and carefully, to keep those air bubbles suspended in the mixture. This is what gives a chiffon its characteristic airy texture. Fold the two components together in wide strokes until there are only a few streaks remaining. Gently transfer the light pink filling into your prepared crust, smoothing out the surface evenly. Let cool at room temperature for one hour before moving the pie into your fridge. Chill for at least four hours before slicing.

Right before serving, top with a thin layer of whipped coconut cream over the entire pie, or artful dollops on each slice.

YOGURT PARFAIT TARTLETTES

Makes 12 Servings

Plump berries glitter atop refreshing vanilla-infused yogurt panna cottas, nestled cozily into individual cereal cups. Healthier than your average custard pie but still certain to satisfy your sweet tooth, it's easy to justify going for seconds . . . and maybe even thirds.

1 Blind-Baked Crunchy Cereal Crust (page 40) in 12 Standard Muffin Cups

Yogurt Panna Cotta:
1 Cup Plain Non-Dairy Milk

2½ Teaspoons Agar Powder
3 Cups Plain Vegan Yogurt
⅔ Cup Granulated Sugar
1½ Teaspoons Vanilla Extract

To Finish:
1 Cup Mixed Fresh Berries (Raspberries, Strawberries, Blueberries, Blackberries, or Any of Your Other Favorites)

To make the yogurt panna cotta, vigorously whisk together the non-dairy milk and agar in a medium saucepan, beating thoroughly to break up any potential clumps. Turn on the heat to medium and continue whisking every few minutes. When the liquid seems to thicken a bit and bubbles form around the edges, add in the yogurt and sugar. Stir continuously to introduce the new ingredients and prevent the yogurt from scorching on the bottom. When bubbles break regularly all over the surface, turn off the heat, and add the vanilla. Stir to combine.

While the mixture is still very loose, quickly but carefully pour equal amounts into each baked mini crust. Do not disturb the pans for at least an hour, until the filling cools completely and sets up. At that point, you can move the pans into the fridge and chill the tartlettes thoroughly.

When ready to serve, pop out as many tartlettes as you'd like to serve and top generously with fresh berries.

SWEET CORN CRÈME BRÛLÉE TARTLETTES

*Makes 12
Servings*

Snatching a fresh ear of corn at the height of summer and taking a bite of the raw kernels is one of the greatest culinary pleasures in life. So sweet, so juicy, it feels like a crime to do much more than just eat such flawless corn straight. Of course, it's a different story altogether if you somehow manage to over-purchase, ending up with a glut of perfect corn in need of attention, ASAP. I simply couldn't help exploring other possibilities after stumbling across a particularly sweet batch, which lent itself perfectly to a more dessert-like final destination. Simplicity was the key here to allow those flawless ears to remain firmly in the spotlight. Creamy corn custard brings out its full, fresh flavor, and a brûléed topping makes each tiny tart even more fun to eat than straight off the cob.

1 Unbaked and Unrolled Classic
    Crust (page 36)

Fresh Corn Pudding:
2 Tablespoons Non-Dairy Margarine

1½ Cup Sweet Yellow Corn Kernels,
    Fresh or Frozen and Thawed
½ Cup Granulated sugar
½ Teaspoon Salt
⅛ Teaspoon Cayenne Pepper

1 Cup Canned Full-Fat Coconut Milk
2 Tablespoons Cornstarch

To Serve:
12 Teaspoons Granulated Sugar

Preheat your oven to 325 degrees.

On a lightly floured surface, roll out the pie dough to about ⅛ inch thick. Cut out a dozen 5-inch circles with a cookie cutter, and gently ease the pieces into twelve 4-inch round mini tart molds. Remove any excess, if needed. Line each one with a small scrap of parchment paper and fill with pie weights. Bake for about 15 minutes, until the pastry feels dry, before removing the weights and papers and returning the tarts to the oven. Bake for an additional 5–9 minutes until the crusts are golden brown. Let cool.

Meanwhile, you can begin working on the pudding by heating up the margarine in a medium-sized skillet over moderate heat. Once melted, add the corn kernels and toss to coat. Sauté the corn for about 5 minutes, until it begins to smell irresistible. Stir in the sugar and cook for another 5–8 minutes, until the kernels just begin to brown and caramelize. Mix in the salt and cayenne pepper last.

Place the coconut milk and cornstarch in your blender or food processor. Introduce the caramelized corn as well, and turn the machine on at high speed. Thoroughly puree, until completely smooth; strain through a fine sieve if necessary.

Continued on page 118.

Transfer the mixture to a medium saucepan, cooking over moderate heat and whisking periodically as it comes up to temperature. Bring to a boil, and once it reaches a lively bubble and has thickened significantly, immediately turn off the heat.

Distribute the hot pudding equally between your blind-baked tartlette shells, smoothing out the tops so that they're as perfectly flat as possible. This will allow you to achieve a more even brûlée later on. Cool to room temperature before chilling in the fridge for at least 2 hours.

Only prepare the brûlée topping right before serving. Sprinkle 1 teaspoon of the remaining sugar over the top of each tartlette, evenly blanketing the entire surface. Use a kitchen torch or place the ramekins under a hot broiler set to high, and cook until the sugar turns golden brown, bubbles all over, and caramelizes. Serve immediately.

FROZEN PIES

ACAI BOWL PIES

Makes 12 Servings

Once the superfood of the hour, the acai berry is no longer creating quite such a stir on the health food scene, but has now crossed over to the dessert side. Though naturally quite tart and bitter, those contrasting flavors add incredible depth to otherwise one-note sweet fruits, like bananas and apples. Seen time and again in acai bowls, this unbeatable combination is blended into the consistency of an ultra-thick smoothie, almost like a fruit-based soft serve ice cream. Frozen ahead of time in this revamped rendition, only a matter of seconds will stand between you and sweet relief on steamy summer days.

1 Blind-Baked Crunchy Cereal
　Crust (page 40) Pressed into 12
　Standard Muffin Tins

Acai Smoothie Filling:
2 Large Ripe Bananas (10 Ounces,
　Peeled)

1 Teaspoon Lemon Juice
7 Ounces Frozen Acai Puree, Thawed
½ Cup 100% Apple Juice
¼ Cup Light Agave Nectar
⅛ Teaspoon Salt

To Finish:
1–2 Large Ripe Bananas, Thinly
　Sliced
½–⅔ Cup Granola
3–4 Tablespoons Vegan Honey-
　Flavored Syrup (page 73) or
　Brown Rice Syrup

Just like the standard acai bowl itself, these frozen berry mini pies just take a little bit of planning and a good blender. Toss all of the filling ingredients into the blender and thoroughly puree. Pause to scrape down the sides if necessary, until the mixture is completely smooth.

Leaving the prepared pie shells right in the muffin tins, distribute the purple puree evenly between them, filling each one just about to the top. Smooth out the surfaces with a spatula before moving the muffin tins to a level surface in your freezer. Let rest, undisturbed, for at least 4–6 hours or until frozen solid.

When ready to enjoy, pop out as many little pies as you'd like to serve and let thaw at room temperature for 10–15 minutes before serving. Meanwhile, top with sliced bananas, granola, and syrup as desired. Dig in when soft enough to easily bite.

BLOOD ORANGE CREAMSICLE PIE

Serves 8–12

Citrus fruits are just about the only thing keeping me sane through the cold, harsh months of winter. Shattering the gray days with their vibrant hues and bold, tart flavors, all variety of lemons, grapefruits, and of course oranges are absolute staples when little other fresh produce can be found. Blood oranges top that list of favorites, thanks to their more nuanced flavor and inherent sweetness, not to mention the obviously striking crimson color. Though delicious enough to satisfy when eaten out of hand, it's a real treat to take that flavor a bit further. Blended up in a rich, creamy filling and frozen to a sliceable consistency, it's reminiscent of those iconic creamsicle smoothies from mall kiosks, but all grown up. No matter how chilly those dark days get, it's still never too cold for this frozen pie.

1 Blind-Baked Graham Cracker Crust
   (page 48) or Vanilla Cookie Crust
   (page 48)

Creamsicle Filling:
1 12-Ounce Aseptic Package Extra-
   Firm Silken Tofu

1 Pound (About 3) Blood Oranges,
   Zested, Peeled and Seeded
½ Cup Canned Full-Fat Coconut
   Milk
¾ Cup Granulated Sugar
1½ Teaspoons Vanilla Extract
⅛ Teaspoon Salt
2 Tablespoons Olive Oil

3 Tablespoons Cornstarch
1 Tablespoon Vodka (Optional)

To Finish:
1–2 Blood Oranges, Peeled, Seeded,
   and Sliced Crosswise
Fresh Mint Leaves (Optional)

To bring this pie together, start by draining away as much excess liquid from the tofu as possible. Break it up into rough chunks, and drop them into the bowl of your food processor or blender. Add the zest and blood oranges, separating the segments so that the pieces are easier to incorporate. Pour in the coconut milk, then secure the lid and pulse to get things moving. When it appears that the blades can easily reach everything, puree thoroughly, until completely smooth. Pause to scrape down the sides of the bowl if you see any sneaky chunks sticking to the walls, refusing to be blended.

Add in the remaining filling ingredients and blend until the mixture is homogeneous. Transfer to a medium saucepan and set on moderate heat, stirring periodically and being especially careful to scrape the bottom of the pan to prevent burning. Cook until the liquid reaches a full, rolling boil and is significantly thickened in consistency. Immediately turn off the heat , stir in the vodka (if using, for a creamier texture when frozen), and pour into your prepared crust.

Cool to room temperature, undisturbed, before carefully moving the pie to a flat surface in your freezer. Let rest for at least 6–8 hours before serving, but even longer is better.

Just prior to slicing, garnish with sliced rounds of blood oranges and fresh mint, if desired.

HULA PIE

*Makes 10–12
Servings*

Macadamia nuts are a luxurious delicacy frequently associated with Hawaii, so imagine my surprise when I discovered that like so many other plants and animals on the islands, they too were imports. Actually originating in Australia, sadly few working macadamia nut plantations still exist in the Aloha State. That small detail sure doesn't stop gift shops from stocking macadamia souvenirs by the dozens, or restaurants from sprinkling them over every dish from appetizer to dessert. Thus, my inspiration for this "Hawaiian" pie comes from a Waikiki eatery catering more to visitors than locals. Regardless, the appeal of an ice cream pie topped with fudge sauce and crunchy mac nuts is undeniable, and it was effortless to get roped into the tropical illusion. My rendition throws a bit more island flavor into the mix, with accents of coconut and pineapple throughout. This is what paradise tastes like to me.

1 Blind-Baked Chocolate Cookie
   Crust (page 48)
Tropical Macadamia Filling:
1 Cup Roasted, Unsalted Macadamia
   Nuts, Divided
1 Cup Canned Full-Fat Coconut Milk

½ Cup Canned Crushed Pineapple,
   Drained
⅓ Cup Light Agave Nectar
2 Teaspoons Vanilla Extract
⅓ Cup Coconut Oil, Melted
½ Teaspoon Salt

To Finish:
½ Cup Salted Chocolate Fudge Sauce
   (page 65)
½ Cup Roasted, Unsalted Macadamia
   Nuts, Halved

First things first, measure out ¼ cup of the macadamia nuts from the filling and finely chop them. Set aside for the time being.

Take the remaining nuts and place them in the canister of your blender, along with the coconut milk. Begin blending on low speed, just to break down the macadamias a bit. They're a softer nut than most, so there's no need to soak them unless your blender is truly underpowered. Allow a few extra minutes of processing for a less powerful machine. Add the pineapple, agave, and vanilla next, starting on low speed but gradually cranking it up to the highest setting. Let blend for a solid 3–4 minutes, until the mixture is silky-smooth.

When absolutely no lumps remain, keep the motor running while slowly streaming in the melted coconut oil, just like you would to emulsify a dressing. Don't rush the process; it might take another two minutes to drizzle the entire measure in. Finally add the salt and pulse briefly to incorporate.

Mix in the reserved macadamia nuts by hand, to distribute them throughout the mixture, before transferring it to your prepared crust. Carefully move the whole pie to a flat surface in your freezer. Let freeze until solidified; at least 8 hours.

Right before serving, gently warm the fudge sauce so that it's easily pourable, and flood the top of the pie with as much chocolate as the crust can hold. Sprinkle with the final measure of macadamia nuts, slice, and devour.

KAHLUA PIE

*Makes 8–12
Servings*

My mom's kahlua pie is the stuff of legends among family members, the sort of dessert that rarely makes an appearance on the table but frequently peppers conversations about sweets. Everyone loves it, coffee fanatics and fair-weather drinkers alike. Even as a child of no more than 5 or 6, well before I understood a thing about caffeine or alcohol content, I remember stealing forkfuls off of others' plates with glee. What's not to love about a creamy custard pie, lightened with whipped cream and spiked liberally with a shot or two (or three) of kahlua? With just enough bitterness from the coffee to keep it from going over the edge, it's the kind of grand finale that you can always find room for.

My ice box rendition harkens more to coffee ice cream than boozy pudding, but make no mistake, that frosty filling still packs a real punch of alcohol.

1 Blind-Baked Graham Cracker Crust (page 48), Vanilla Cookie Crust (page 48), or Chocolate Cookie Crust (page 48)

Kahlua Custard Filling:
1 Cup Plain Non-Dairy Milk

¼ Cup Granulated Sugar
1 Tablespoon Cornstarch
2 Teaspoons Arrowroot
1 Tablespoon Instant Coffee Powder
⅓ Cup Kahlua or Other Coffee
  Liqueur

1 Batch Meringue, Unbaked (page 54)

To Finish:
2 Tablespoons Natural Cocoa Powder

In a medium-sized saucepan, whisk together the non-dairy milk, sugar, cornstarch, arrowroot, instant coffee, and kahlua. Yes, by incorporating the liqueur so early in the game, some of the alcohol will inevitably cook out, but in this case that's a good thing. That much alcohol would taste harsh and sharp without some time to mellow on the stove.

Beat vigorously to work out any lumps of starch, then set the saucepan on the stove over medium heat. Stir occasionally as the mixture cooks, taking care to scrape along the sides and bottom to prevent scorching. Once the liquid is steadily bubbling and has thickened significantly, turn off the heat and let cool to room temperature before proceeding.

When filling has cooled, prepare the meringue according to the recipe until you reach the baking instructions. Transfer the cooked custard to a large bowl and stir in a dollop of the fluffy meringue. This first introduction is just going to lighten the custard slightly, so it's okay if you knock all the bubbles out of the meringue. From here on in though, gently fold the two components together using a wide spatula, preserving as many of those air pockets as possible. Fold in the

Continued on page 130.

remaining meringue in three separate additions, mixing until no longer streaky. Pour the filling into your prepared crust, smoothing down the top with a spatula.

Carefully move the pie onto a flat surface in the freezer, to rest until frozen solid. This should be at least 6 hours of undisturbed time in the chill chest, but waiting overnight will be your best bet.

Right before serving, lightly sprinkle the entire surface with sifted cocoa powder. For a deluxe presentation, center a clean paper doily on the pie top, sprinkle cocoa powder over doily, then carefully remove doily to reveal a lacy pattern.

If there's more filling than will fit into the crust, tuck it into an individual ramekin, freeze, and call it a "frozen soufflé."

MALTED STRAWBERRY MILKSHAKE PIE

Makes 8-12 Servings

For someone who missed out entirely on the era of the soda shoppe, I sure do get the most curious cravings for tall, frosty malted milkshakes. For a solid summer, back in my wild youth, I recall mixing up a different flavored shake almost every day, powering through a full pound of malt powder in the process. Now, malt without milk powder is a bit harder to come by, but malted barley syrup scratches that same itch quite nicely, adding a comforting syrupy sweetness at the same time. Vanilla malts will always reign in popularity, but an unlikely combination that caught hold of my taste buds was malt and strawberries. Light and fruity while simultaneously tasting rich and toasty, it breathes fresh life into the tried-and-true concept for a new generation.

1 Unbaked Chocolate Cookie Crust (page 48) or Vanilla Cookie Crust (page 48)
Malted Strawberry Ice Cream:
1 Pound Strawberries, Fresh or Frozen and Thawed

2½ Cups Vanilla or Plain Non-Dairy Milk
⅓ Cup Malted Barley Syrup
¾ Cup Granulated Sugar
2 Tablespoons Arrowroot
¼ Teaspoon Salt

1 Tablespoon Vanilla Extract
To Finish:
Whipped Coconut Cream (page 52) (Optional)
Sliced Fresh Strawberries

If using fresh strawberries, begin by washing, drying, and hulling them. Place the berries into your blender and thoroughly puree. Pause to scrape down the sides of the canister to ensure that even the smallest, clingiest chunks are incorporated, and allow up to 5 minutes for the blades to work out all the lumps. Pass the liquefied strawberries through a fine mesh strainer to catch any tricky seeds, pressing to get out all of the liquid and discarding the solids left over. You should have approximately 1⅔ cups of smooth puree at this stage.

Pour the strawberry puree into a medium saucepan, along with the non-dairy milk, malted barley syrup, sugar, arrowroot, and salt. Whisk vigorously to break up any lumps of starch and combine all of the other ingredients. Once smooth, turn on the heat to medium, and begin whisking gently as it comes up to temperature. When the liquid has significantly thickened and bubbles are breaking rapidly on the surface, remove the pan from the stove. Whisk in the vanilla and let cool to room temperature.

Transfer the ice cream base to the fridge and chill thoroughly before churning; at least 4 hours. When chilled all the way through, use your ice cream maker to churn the mixture according to the manufacturer's instructions. Have your

Continued on page 133.

prepared pie crust at the ready and immediately transfer the finished ice cream into it. Smooth over the top with your spatula, then stash the pie in your freezer to allow it to set up more solidly. Make sure it's resting on a flat surface, and let it "cure" for a bare minimum of 6 hours before slicing. If you can spare the time, giving it an overnight freeze will yield the cleanest cuts.

To serve, top slices with dollops of whipped coconut cream and additional fresh berries, if desired.

Malted Peanut Butter and Jelly Pie: Speaking of classic combinations, this variation brings the much-loved PB & J sandwich back into the realm of dessert. You've already got the essence of jelly through the strawberry filling, so just introduce a generous handful of chopped peanuts to pay homage to the peanut butter. Simply add ½–⅔ cup of chopped, roasted and lightly salted peanuts into the ice cream within the final 5 minutes of churning, and proceed as previously instructed.

MOJITO PIE

Makes 8–10 Servings

If a mojito on the rocks is poured *over* ice, what do you call a mojito *made of* ice? No, that's not some terrible riddle with a trick answer, but a uniquely refreshing and intoxicating dessert. Straight out of the icebox, each rum-spiked wedge remains impossibly light and creamy, owing to the richness of avocado. Just like the chilled beverage, even non-drinkers will find it effortless to down one or two on a hot day.

1 Unbaked Graham Cracker Crust (page 48) or Vanilla Cookie Crust (page 48) in a 9-Inch Round Springform Pan

Mojito Filling:
1 Ripe Medium-Size Avocado

¼ Cup Lime Juice
Zest from 1 Large Lime (About 1½ Teaspoons)
¾ Cup Light Agave Nectar
½ Cup Vegan Sour Cream
1 6-Ounce Container (¾ Cup) Plain Vegan Yogurt

¼ Cup White Rum
½ Teaspoon Peppermint Extract
⅛ Teaspoon Salt

To Finish:
Whipped Coconut Cream (page 52)

This no-bake icebox pie comes together in a flash. Begin by pressing the graham cracker crust mixture into the bottom of a 9-inch round springform pan and about 1½ inches up the sides. Place the pan in the freezer to let it solidify.

Meanwhile, pit and peel the avocado and toss the flesh into your food processor along with the lime juice and zest. Thoroughly puree, pausing after about a minute of blending, to scrape down the sides of the bowl with your spatula. Add in the agave, "sour cream," and yogurt, pureeing again until completely smooth. For the final addition, incorporate the rum, peppermint extract, and salt together with a few quick pulses.

Transfer the pale green filling to your prepared crust, smoothing out the top evenly by giving the whole pan a few gentle taps on the counter. Place the pan back in your freezer, being careful to set it on a flat, stable area—don't attempt any crazy balancing acts on top of the frozen peas here! Trust me, scraping ice-hard pie filling out of the freezer is not a fun task.

Allow the filling to freeze, undisturbed, for at least two hours before applying the coconut whipped cream on top in a swirled fashion. Either serve right away, or keep the pie stashed in the freezer for up to 2 weeks, until you're ready to dig in.

PERSIMMON CHIFFON PIE

Makes 8–10 Servings

Persimmons, fickle fruits that they are, come in two official varieties, but two unofficial categories: Super-sweet, or tart enough to pucker your lips for hours to come. Anyone who has mistakenly interpreted bright color as an indicator of ripeness can attest just how the dreadful taste of a hard, sour persimmon can linger on the palate. Understandably, some are turned off by this small window of delicious perfection, but it's truly a gamble worth taking. Fuyu persimmons, round on the bottom much like an orange tomato, become so soft and jelly-like when ready that they typically can't be eaten out of hand. They shine in the kitchen, where their full potential can be unlocked with only light manipulation. While the pulp can get a bit gooey raw, frozen to a sliceable consistency still as soft as ice cream, you can sidestep all of the pitfalls for a risk-free persimmon experience.

1 Blind-Baked Vanilla Cookie Crust (page 48) or Graham Cracker Crust (page 48)
1 14-Ounce Can Full-Fat Coconut Milk, Chilled for at Least 2 Hours

¼ Cup Water
1½ Teaspoons Agar Powder
1½ Cups Fuyu Persimmon Pulp*
1 Cup Granulated Sugar

1¾ Teaspoons Five-Spice Powder (page 12)
1 Tablespoon Non-Dairy Margarine, Melted
½ Teaspoon Vanilla Extract

Without shaking or jostling the can, remove the coconut milk from the fridge and pop it open. Use a large spoon to carefully scoop out only the thick, almost solid white cream which should have risen to the top, leaving the thinner liquid underneath behind. Reserve it for another use or discard. Plop the coconut cream into the bowl of your stand mixer and beat with the whisk attachment until light, fluffy, and somewhat increased in volume. Set aside.

Disperse the agar powder in the water, stirring to ensure that there are no clumps, before transferring it to a medium-sized microwave-safe container. Heat at full power for 20–45 seconds, until bubbling vigorously. Quickly mix in the persimmon pulp, sugar, and five-spice. Return it to the microwave and heat for 2–3 minutes, pausing every 60 seconds to stir.

Once bubbles are breaking all over the surface and not just around the edges, pull it out and quickly mix in the melted margarine and vanilla. Add a small spoonful of the whipped coconut cream to lighten the mixture a bit. Introduce the remaining cream in two separate additions, using a wide spatula to gently fold the two mixtures together, rather than stirring roughly. The idea is to keep the cream as light and fluffy as possible while incorporating the persimmon gel.

When the filling is homogeneous, pour it into your prepared crust, and let cool completely before disturbing it again. The agar base must reach room temperature before hitting the icebox in order to set up properly.

Place on a flat surface in your freezer and allow at least 8–10 hours for the pie to freeze solidly before serving.

*Depending on the size of your persimmons, this measure will require between 3 to 4 fruits. Only when the flesh yields readily to gentle pressure and the persimmons smell vaguely sweet and floral, when they're as ripe as can be, should you plan to prepare the pulp. Use a paring knife to cut out the center crown of leaves and use your finger to peel away the skin if it's particularly thick. In many cases, you can just turn the persimmons upside down and squeeze out the innards like a tube of toothpaste. Puree the flesh in either a food processor or blender until smooth.

Easy as Vegan Pie

RAW EGGNOG PIE

Makes 10–14 Servings

It may not make it past the raw food police, but for a whole food treat that needs no heat, a more impressive holiday pie can't be found. Zero eggs but plenty of nog flavor, rich pistachios, and coconut milk are what carry the unique taste, aided by more unusual additions such as miso and black salt for a more umami, slightly egg-y essence. Fresh, pungent nutmeg is the key to finishing on a high note, so if possible, seek out fresh, whole nutmeg and grate it straight over individual slices upon serving.

1 Rawesome Fruit and Nut Crust (page 49)

Raw Eggnog Filling:
½ Cup Canned Full-Fat Coconut Milk
1 Cup Raw Pistachios, Soaked for 4–6 Hours and Drained
½ Cup Light Agave Nectar
1 Tablespoon Vanilla Extract

1 Teaspoon Sweet White Miso Paste
½ Teaspoon Ground Cinnamon
½ Teaspoon Ground Nutmeg
½ Teaspoon Black Salt (Kala Namak)
6 Tablespoons Coconut Oil, Melted

Creamy Cashew Topping:
1 Cup Raw Cashews, Soaked for 4–6 Hours and Drained

½ Cup Canned Full-Fat Coconut Milk
¼ Cup Grade B Maple Syrup
1 Teaspoon Vanilla Extract

To Finish:
Ground Nutmeg

It's very handy, but not mandatory, to have a high-speed blender to power through this nut-heavy recipe. If using a standard blender, be a bit more patient with the process, as it could take 5–10 additional minutes to attain the same sort of texture. Begin by placing the coconut milk, pistachios, agave, vanilla, miso paste, spices, and salt in the canister of the blender, and begin pureeing on low. Allow the blades to begin breaking down the nuts, before gradually increasing the speed all the way up to the highest setting.

Blend for two minutes, until the largest chunks have become incorporated and the mixture is looking fairly liquid. Continue blending while slowly drizzling in the melted coconut oil to fully emulsify the fat. Allow another 2–3 minutes of pureeing on high, pausing to scrape down the sides of the canister if needed, until the filling is perfectly smooth. Pour into your prepared crust and let sit for 15 minutes before moving the whole thing onto a flat surface in your freezer.

Meanwhile, you can move on to the topping. Thoroughly rinse and dry your blender before starting to load it up again. Combine all the cashew topping ingredients, and as before, begin blending on low until the nuts are mostly broken down. Slowly increase the speed until you reach the fastest setting, and allow it to keep pulverizing the mixture for up to 5 full minutes, until flawlessly smooth. You can either transfer the topping to the pie now, smoothing it over the top evenly, or set it aside in the fridge to dollop on separate slices later.

Let the pie rest in the freezer for at least 6 hours or overnight. To serve, sprinkle with freshly ground nutmeg.

ROOT BEER FLOAT PIE

Makes 8–10 Servings

It's ironic that the foods we most closely identify with America, such as burgers and apple pie, are actually imports from other countries. Just like the largely immigrant-based population itself, our most cherished staples have in fact come from somewhere else. One thing that we can truly claim as our own, though, is root beer. Nowhere else on earth will you find this flavor, unless it's being served as a specialty of American cuisine. There are far worse legacies to bear, even if it's technically not a full-fledged food. Though wonderful all by itself, vanilla ice cream was the best thing to ever happen to root beer, bonding to create a soda shoppe float far greater than the sum of its parts. Of course, we have many other ancient civilizations to thank for the invention of ice cream, too.

1 Unbaked Chocolate Cookie Crust
   (page 48)
Root Beer Pudding:
1 Cup Regular Root Beer Soda (Not
   Diet or Sugar-Free)

1 Cup Vanilla or Plain Vegan Creamer
½ Cup Granulated Sugar
2 Tablespoons Cornstarch
2 Teaspoons Arrowroot Powder
1 Tablespoon Root Beer Extract

Pinch Salt
To Finish:
1 Batch Triple Vanilla Ice Cream
   (page 64)

To make the root beer layer, combine everything from soda to salt in a medium saucepan, thoroughly whisking to make sure there are no lumps of starch remaining. Cook over moderate heat, stirring occasionally, just until it comes to a boil. Turn off the heat and pour the hot pudding into your prepared pie crust. Let cool completely, until softly set, before transferring the whole pie to a flat surface in your freezer. Allow at least 6–8 hours for it to freeze solidly before topping it off with vanilla ice cream.

If churning the ice cream fresh, simply smooth it over the root beer layer rather than packing it into an airtight container. If using previously churned and frozen ice cream, soften it slightly by microwaving for just 10–15 seconds, so that it can be spread more easily. Once evenly distributed over the first layer, tuck your pie back into the freezer for a minimum of 3 hours before slicing and serving.

Go ahead, give yourself a break! To speed up prep and cut down on hassle, you have my permission to buy a quart of vegan vanilla ice cream from the store. Many brands now have rich, creamy formulas tempting enough to win over the most discerning tasters, so the quality of your pie won't suffer one bit.

SPUMONI PIE

*Makes 10–14
Servings*

Made up of gloriously bold stripes in green, pink, and brown, the Italian spumoni (or spumone, depending on who's telling the story) has never been much for subtlety. Bearing equally intense pistachio, cherry, and chocolate flavors, part of the fun is the inherent flamboyance of these show-stopping ice cream bombes. Coloring outside of the lines a bit and swirling those immaculate layers seems like a fitting extra bit of flair. The only thing possibly more dramatic will be the rave reviews!

Rawesome Fruit and Nut Crust
  (page 49) or Unbaked Vanilla
  Cookie Crust (page 48)
Creamy Filling:
2 Cups Raw, Shelled Pistachios,
  Soaked for 4–6 Hours and Drained
½ Cup Coconut Oil or Cocoa Butter,
  Melted
½ Cup Light Agave Nectar
1 Sweet Red Apple (Such as Fuji or
  Red Delicious), Peeled, Cored,
  and Chopped

2 Teaspoons Vanilla Extract
2 Teaspoons Lemon Juice
⅛ Teaspoon Salt
Pistachio Swirl:
1 Cup Fresh Baby Spinach, Lightly
  Packed
¼ Teaspoon Almond Extract
Cherry Swirl:
⅓ Cup Raw Cashews, Soaked for 3–6
  Hours, Drained
⅔ Cup Frozen and Thawed Dark
  Cherries

2 Tablespoons Light Agave Nectar
Chocolate Swirl:
⅓ Cup Natural Cocoa Powder
2 Tablespoons Water
To Finish:
Whipped Coconut Cream (page 52)
Fresh Cherries

The creamy filling is the base that will support all three flavors—the good news is that it comes together in a snap. Simply toss the ingredients into your blender and turn it up to the highest setting you've got. Thoroughly puree until smooth all the way through, pausing to scrape down the sides of the canister with a spatula as needed. If you don't have a high-speed blender, this could take upwards of 10 minutes, so be patient and keep those blades spinning.

Once perfectly pureed, transfer half of the filling to a medium-sized bowl. Add the spinach and almond extract into the blender with the remaining half, and blend until bright green and completely smooth once more. This will make up the pistachio swirl, which is really more like the base since it takes up more of the filling. Set aside.

Rinse out and thoroughly dry the canister of your blender before returning your attention to the bowl of filling. Moving along to the cherry swirl, pour half of that filling back into the blender, along with cashews, cherries, and agave. Let it rip and puree until creamy and lump-free. Set aside.

Whisk the cocoa and water into remaining filling. Be patient as it may take a bit of elbow grease to incorporate all of the dry powder. Finally, your chocolate swirl is ready to go and you can start assembling the pie.

Pull out your prepared crust and add dollops of each swirl flavor, randomly distributing them in the pan until all are used up. Run a long toothpick or wooden skewer through the center of the pie, reaching down to the bottom, in gentle circular motions to marble all three components together.

Place the pie in your freezer on a flat surface and let chill until solidly frozen. Wait 6 hours at minimum, but longer to be safe.

Smooth an even layer of whipped coconut cream over the top just before slicing, and serve with a handful of fresh cherries alongside, if desired.

WINTER WONDERLAND PEPPERMINT PIE

Makes 10–12
Servings

Counterintuitive though it may be, as soon as the first fluffy white flakes of snow begin to fall each winter, I find myself ferociously craving peppermint. The cold chill might send me running for sweaters, but I'll tough out the shivers for that refreshing, sweet flavor that seems to sparkle just like the fresh snow. Let the mint shine though in this festive pie, supported by a base bearing the essence of white chocolate and full-bodied vanilla. Sprinkled liberally with crushed peppermint candies, it really is a beautiful sight.

1 Baked Vanilla Cookie Crust (page 48) or Graham Cracker Crust (page 48)

Peppermint Candy Filling:
2 Cups Plain Vegan Creamer
½ Cup Light Agave Nectar
3 Tablespoons Cornstarch

¼ Teaspoon Salt
6 Tablespoons (3 Ounces) Pure Cocoa Butter, Chopped
2 Teaspoons Vanilla Extract
½ Teaspoon Peppermint Extract
2 6-Ounce Containers (1 ½ Cups) Vanilla Vegan Yogurt

4 Ounces Peppermint Starlight Candies (About 20), Crushed
To Finish:
5 Peppermint Starlight Candies, Crushed

In a medium-sized saucepan, whisk together the creamer, agave, cornstarch, and salt. Beat vigorously to break up any lumps of starch and ensure a smooth custard base later on. Set over medium heat, and stir occasionally as the mixture cooks. Once significantly thickened and at a rolling boil, turn down the heat to low and add in the chunks of cocoa butter. Stir slowly to incorporate and allow the pieces to melt in smoothly, scraping the bottom and sides of the pan to prevent anything from sticking and scorching.

When the cocoa butter has seemingly disappeared, turn off the heat and add in the vanilla along with the peppermint extract. Let the cooked custard cool for about 20 minutes before whisking in the yogurt, stirring until homogeneous. Allow the mixture to stand until it reaches room temperature before sprinkling in the crushed peppermint candies. Fold to distribute the pieces evenly throughout, but don't fuss with it too much because extra agitation will cause the candies to dissolve. You want to keep some nice crunchy bites intact here!

Pour the filling into your waiting crust, and place the whole pie into the freezer on a flat surface. Let freeze for at least 6 hours, but ideally overnight, before serving.

Right before slicing, sprinkle the remaining crushed peppermint candies evenly over the frozen surface of the pie. Cut into wedges and prepare for a refreshing minty rush!

NUT PIES

CARAMEL MACADAMIA CRUMB TART

Makes 10–14 Servings

Messy foods are often avoided for important dining occasions, but I'm here to argue that they're actually among the best options. They strip away the pretense of being polite, proper, or restrained, unburdening the eater from an etiquette straightjacket. When you've got sticky caramel dripping down your fork and it's all you can do to prevent yourself from bathing in it, who really cares about which side of the plate the glasses should go on, or if you're sitting up straight? Downright luxurious with a crumb topping to crown the expanse of whole macadamia nuts, forget about taking dainty bites and dig in already! Sorry in advance about the dry cleaning bill.

1 Blind-Baked Vanilla Cookie Crust (Page 48) or Graham Cracker Crust (Page 48)

Gooey Caramel-Macadamia Filling:
1 Cup Granulated Sugar
2 Tablespoons Light Corn Syrup or Light Agave Nectar
2 Tablespoons Water

½ Teaspoon Salt
¼ Cup Canned Full-Fat Coconut Milk
¼ Cup Non-Dairy Margarine
1 Teaspoon Vanilla Extract
2 Cups Whole Roasted and Unsalted Macadamia Nuts

Crumb Topping:
¼ Cup Non-Dairy Margarine
¼ Cup Granulated Sugar
¼ Teaspoon Salt
¼ Teaspoon Vanilla Extract
¾ Cup All-Purpose Flour

Preheat your oven to 375 degrees.

For the topping, cream together the margarine and sugar either in the bowl of your stand mixer or simply in a medium bowl with a sturdy fork. When homogeneous and slightly fluffy, add in the salt, vanilla, and flour. It may take some serious elbow grease to combine these elements by hand, but resist the temptation to add water! After a bit of time, the dry goods will become incorporated into a crumbly mixture of larger and smaller pieces. Set aside.

For the caramel, pull out a medium saucepan and bring the sugar, corn syrup or agave, water, and salt to a boil over medium-high heat. Stir only once to combine, and then refrain from using your spatula again until the very end. After the mixture reaches a boil, reduce the heat slightly, but continue to cook, swirling the pan to keep the ingredients mixing evenly, until the syrup reaches a deep amber color. Standing back slightly in case the hot sugar sputters or splatters, carefully add the coconut milk, followed by the margarine, vanilla, and salt. Stir until the margarine fully melts and the mixture is smooth. Immediately turn off the heat, and let stand for 5 minutes before stirring in the macadamia nuts.

Transfer the caramel filling into your crust and quickly scatter the crumb topping evenly all over. Bake for 20–25 minutes, until the crumbs are brown and the caramel bubbly. Let cool completely before serving but do NOT refrigerate! Cold caramel is very hard to slice, and not nearly as much fun to eat.

CHESTNUT CRUNCH PIE

Serves 10–12

For as few holiday traditions as we keep in my family, the ones we do hold close are absolutely unshakable. If, for example, we didn't throw at least a few fresh chestnuts on the still smoldering embers of our single yearly conflagration in the fireplace, I don't know if the entire winter season would truly count. Emerging lightly charred and smoking hot, we sit around chatting as a family, cracking the chestnuts out of their shells and popping the rich, creamy centers in our mouths. The odd nut that won't crack or turns out dry doesn't dampen our spirits; back into the fire the rotten few go, along with the spent shells, coaxing the hungry flame to return. The nutty smell of the fire permeates the whole house, and eventually, when it's time to turn in for bed, I have chestnut-flavored dreams. Attempting to condense that fond memory down to a single bite provided the inspiration for a truly unparalleled pie. Shaking up the texture with custard, chunks of roasted chestnuts and abundant pieces of cacao crunch make up the heart and soul of what may just become a new annual custom.

1 Blind-Baked Chocolate Cookie
    Crust (page 48)
Candied Cacao Crunch:
⅓ Cup Granulated Sugar
1 Tablespoon Water
1 Tablespoon Light Corn Syrup or
    Light Agave Nectar
⅛ Teaspoon Salt
⅔ Cup Cacao Nibs

Chestnut Custard:
¼ Cup Non-Dairy Margarine
¼ Cup Granulated Sugar
⅛ Teaspoon Salt
2 Cups (About 10 Ounces) Roasted
    and Peeled Whole Chestnuts
1½ Cups Plain Non-Dairy Milk
½ Cup Dark Brown Sugar, Firmly
    Packed

½ Whole Vanilla Bean, Split and
    Scraped or 2 Teaspoons Vanilla
    Extract
3 Tablespoons Cornstarch
¼ Teaspoon Ground Cinnamon

To Finish:
Whipped Coconut Cream (Optional)

    The cacao crunch is easy to make, but needs time to cool and fully set, so that should be the first order of business. Pull out a baking sheet and line it with a silpat or piece of parchment paper; set aside.

    Set a small saucepan over medium-low heat. Combine the sugar, water, corn syrup or agave, and salt, and bring the mixture up to a vigorous bubble. Do not stir again from this point forward, gently swirling the pan instead to keep the contents well-mixed.

Continued on page 152.

Continue to heat the sugar until it caramelizes and turns amber-brown all over, just at the very brink of burning. Quickly turn off the heat, stir in the cacao nibs, and pour the mixture out onto your prepared baking sheet. While still hot, you can further distribute the nibs a bit to even them out, if desired.

Let cool completely, until firm and brittle. Break into pieces before placing them in your food processor. Lightly pulse until you're left with small pieces that include just one or two whole nibs encased in caramel. Set aside for the time being, thoroughly wiping out your food processor for the next stage.

At this point, preheat your oven to 350 degrees.

To caramelize the chestnuts, begin by melting down the margarine in a medium saucepan over moderate heat. Add in the sugar and salt, and cook until the granules have dissolved. Toss in the chestnuts, cooking until the surrounding syrup turns golden brown and thick enough to coat the chestnuts. Let cool for 15 minutes before transferring to your food processor and pulsing lightly, just 3–5 times. The chestnuts should still be in large pieces at this point. Remove about 1¼ cups of pieces and scatter them in your prepared crust.

To the chestnuts remaining in your food processor, add the milk, brown sugar, vanilla, cornstarch, and cinnamon, pureeing thoroughly. Pause to scrape down the sides of the bowl as needed, until the mixture is smooth.

Transfer the chestnut liquid back into the saucepan and set over moderate heat again. Switch over to a whisk, and whisk periodically as the mixture heats. Cook until the custard reaches a boil and has thickened significantly. Cook for one additional minute before pouring the custard evenly over the chopped chestnuts sitting in the crust. Finally, sprinkle the chopped candied cacao nibs over the top, and let cool completely. After reaching room temperature, transfer to the fridge and chill for at least 2 hours for the custard to fully set.

Serve with a dollop of whipped coconut cream, if desired.

BAKLAVA PIE

Makes 12–14
Servings

Much like the beloved chickpea dip known as hummus, many Mediterranean cultures claim to have invented baklava. Considering its worldwide appeal, that title is certainly something worth fighting over. Found in the pastry cases of Greek diners, Lebanese cafés, and Turkish delis, just for starters, there's surprisingly little variation between recipes despite their diverse origins. After an initial sugar rush, it's all about the ephemeral flaky pastry, rich walnuts, and intense cinnamon essence. Since it's typically baked as one large sheet, why not simply craft it into a pie? Arrange the layers of phyllo to form a bottom and top crust, and before you know it, you've got a full-fledged pie on your hands. No matter what anyone else tries to convince you later on down the road, I promise you, this particular pastry is purely American.

3 Cups (About 1 Pound) Finely Chopped Walnuts, Lightly Toasted

⅓ Cup Dark Brown Sugar, Firmly Packed

1¾ Teaspoons Ground Cinnamon

1 Teaspoon Vanilla Extract

½ Teaspoon Salt

½ Cup + 6 Tablespoons Non-Dairy Margarine, Divided and Melted

¾ Cup Vegan Honey-Flavored Syrup (page 73) or Brown Rice Syrup

2 Teaspoons Lemon Juice

1 1-Pound Package Frozen Phyllo Dough, Thawed

Preheat your oven to 375 degrees and lightly grease a 9-inch diameter deep-dish pie pan.

In a medium-sized bowl, combine the chopped walnuts, brown sugar, cinnamon, vanilla, salt, and ½ cup of the melted margarine. Stir well to distribute all of the ingredients and evenly coat the nuts.

Turning your attention to the phyllo, lay down one thin sheet in the bottom of your prepared pie pan. Don't worry if the pastry hangs over the sides of the dish; it will be neatened up later. Dip into the remaining 6 tablespoons margarine with a pastry brush and lightly brush the newly laid sheet. Top that with another piece of phyllo, brush with more margarine, and repeat until you have 8–10 total layers stacked on top of each other, fully covering the bottom of the pie pan.

Pour all of the sugared walnuts into the pan, smoothing them out into an even layer. Repeat the layering process of phyllo, then margarine, until you have another 8–10 sheets stacked on top. Tuck any wayward edges into the sides of the dish, or simply trim with a sharp pair of kitchen shears.

Continued on page 155.

Combine the syrup and lemon juice in a small saucepan over low heat, loosening it up to a more pourable consistency. Meanwhile, score the top of the phyllo into 12–14 equal slices. Pour the hot syrup all over the pastry, being careful not to let it run over the sides of the pie pan.

Bake for 30–35 minutes until the phyllo is golden and flaky. Let cool completely before serving, but don't let this pie sit around too long; the pastry does become increasingly soggy in a relatively short amount of time.

Trigona Pie: Substitute either almonds or pistachios (or a combination of both, if you're feeling festive) for the walnuts, and maple syrup instead of honey-flavored syrup.

GINGERBREAD WALNUT PIE

Serves 10–12

Gingerbread holds a special place in my heart, but not just any pale cookie or wan spice-flavored latte will do when a craving strikes. It's got to be cake, and the darker and denser, the better. The fact is that I chose my Bat Mitzvah reception venue based entirely on the transcendent gingerbread cake they served. Redolent of molasses and finished with a fluffy halo of whipped cream towering over the plate, it's now all I remember about that meal. It took many years to even consider that any pie might match, let alone surpass, that decadent gingerbread experience. The subtly bitter edge of walnuts pairs perfectly with the brash flavor of molasses, bringing out the best of each ingredient. Every bit as rich and intense as the best cakes, I daresay this pie might be the new gingerbread vehicle of choice.

1 Unbaked Classic Crust (page 36), Wholesome Whole Wheat Crust (page 44), or Chocolate Pastry Crust (page 37)

2 Tablespoons Non-Dairy Margarine, Melted

1 Cup Unsweetened Applesauce
⅔ Cup Granulated Sugar
⅓ Cup Molasses
3 Tablespoons Water
½ Cup All-Purpose Flour
2 Teaspoons Ground Ginger
1 Teaspoon Ground Cinnamon

½ Teaspoon Ground Nutmeg
¼ Teaspoon Ground Cloves
¼ Teaspoon Salt
1 Cup Chopped Raw Walnuts
¾ Cup Raw Walnut Halves

Preheat your oven to 375 degrees.

In a large bowl, mix together the melted margarine, applesauce, sugar, molasses, and water.

Separately, sift the flour and whisk in all of the spices and salt. Pour the liquid mixture into the dry, and whisk just long enough to smooth out any lumps. Add the chopped walnuts and stir to incorporate.

Transfer the filling into your pie pan lined with unbaked crust. Arrange the walnut halves in concentric circles on top. Precision isn't critical, as long as the halves are fairly evenly spaced; the overall result will be impressive no matter what, and any small errors will be easy to overlook when the design is cut into wedges for serving.

Bake for 45–50 minutes, until the crust is lightly browned and the center has firmed up enough that it doesn't slosh about when you gently tap the pan.

Let cool to room temperature before slicing and serving.

HAZELNUT TASSIES

Makes 20–24 Tassies

Though traditionally classified as cookies, tassies strike me as tiny pies with identity crises. Sure, they may sit prominently on many a Christmas cookie platter, but what other cookie bears such a distinct crust-and-filling divide? Reinforced with a tender wheat shell to bear the burden of any gooey, sticky, and delightfully messy stuffing, the concept is perfect for holding on to the roly-poly hazelnut. Coarsely chopped, the nuts swim in a softly set sea of maple gel, contrasting an inherent bitter edge with just the right kiss of sweetness. Go ahead, add them to your next cookie swap if you must; they'll always be small but mighty pies at heart.

Press-in-Pan Mini Crusts:
½ Cup Non-Dairy Margarine
½ Cup (4 Ounces) Vegan Cream
   Cheese
¼ Teaspoon Ground Ginger
1 Cup Whole Wheat Pastry Flour

Maple-Hazelnut Filling:
⅓ Cup Grade B Maple Syrup
⅔ Cup Granulated Sugar
¼ Cup Unsweetened Applesauce
2 Teaspoons Vanilla Extract
¼ Teaspoon Salt

1½ Cups Blanched and Toasted
   Hazelnuts, Very Coarsely
   Chopped

For the dough, first cream together the margarine, cream cheese, and ginger in the bowl of your stand mixer, using the paddle attachment. Beat on medium speed until the mixture is perfectly smooth and homogeneous. Scrape down the bottom and sides of the bowl with your spatula and add the flour, beginning to mix again at a low speed, until the mixture is just combined and a forms a cohesive dough. Pinch off walnut-sized pieces of dough, roll into balls, and drop each one into lightly greased mini muffin cups. Chill the pans for 15 minutes so that the dough is less sticky and easier to manage, then use lightly moistened fingers to press each piece across the bottom of its cup and up the sides.

After forming the tassie shells, loosely cover the pans with plastic wrap and place them in the freezer to chill while you make the filling.

Preheat your oven to 375 degrees.

To prepare the filling, set a small saucepan over medium heat. Introduce the maple syrup, sugar, and applesauce, briefly stirring to combine. Cook until the sugar fully melts and bubbles all over. Let boil for just one minute before quickly turning off the heat and stirring in the salt and hazelnuts.

Retrieve the unbaked mini shells from the freezer and spoon the hot filling into the shells until they are each about three-quarters full. Do not be tempted to top them off, as they can easily overflow and make a big mess of the oven!

Bake for 20–25 minutes until the shells are golden brown and the filling is lightly set.

Allow the tassies to cool for at least 30 minutes before diving in. Serve warm or at room temperature; do not refrigerate or they can become quite tough to bite into. Eat as soon as possible for the best flavor, but the tassies can be stored in airtight containers for up to three days.

MARZIPAN CROSTATA

Makes 8–10 servings

Almond-lovers are a pretty die-hard bunch; practically inhaling them raw, salted, seasoned, sweet, or savory, we agree that there is no wrong way to enjoy an almond. Marzipan ought to be the truest form of this lovable nut, but alas, it's often flavored more with sugar than the roasted aromas of its supposed base ingredient. This particular homemade version of marzipan is quite soft and easy to spread, not to mention considerably less sweet, to prevent it from tasting like pure candy wrapped up in a buttery crust. You don't need to be a fanatic to appreciate the subtle roasted flavor contained within this brilliantly simple freeform pastry.

1 Unbaked and Unrolled Classic
  Crust (Page 36) or Wholesome
  Whole Wheat Crust (Page 44)
Marzipan Filling:
2 Cups Slivered and Blanched
  Almonds, Toasted

⅔ Cup Granulated Sugar
½ Teaspoon Salt
⅓ Cup Plain Vegan Yogurt
¼ Cup Non-Dairy Margarine
½ Teaspoon Almond Extract

To Finish:
Golden Pastry Glaze (page 25)
3–4 Tablespoons Raw Sliced
  Almonds
1–2 Tablespoons Turbinado Sugar

Preheat your oven to 375 degrees and line a sheet pan with a silpat or piece of parchment paper.

To prepare the marzipan, combine the almonds, sugar, and salt in the bowl of your food processor and pulse until finely ground. Introduce the yogurt, pulsing to incorporate. Scrape down the sides of the bowl with your spatula and then process until completely smooth. Be patient as this could take up to 10 minutes, depending on what kind of power your motor is packing. Through the feed shoot, gradually add the margarine about 1 tablespoon a time, running the blades without pause until each addition fully disappears into the mix. When all the margarine has been incorporated, add the almond extract, and pulse to combine.

At this point, you can get your chilled pie dough and roll it out on a lightly floured surface to about ⅛ inch thick, keeping it as round as possible. Gently transfer the dough to your prepared sheet pan.

Scrape the soft marzipan into the very center of the dough circle, spreading it out lightly to within 1–1½ inches of the edge. Gently fold the edges of the dough up and over the filling, keeping it safely contained within.

Lightly brush the exposed edges of crust with the golden pastry glaze before sprinkling evenly with both turbinado sugar and sliced almonds. Move the crostata into the oven and bake for 25–30 minutes, until golden all over. Slide the silpat or parchment paper along with the crostata off the hot sheet and let cool for 15 minutes.

Transfer crostata to a wire rack to allow steam to escape from underneath, and allow at least 10–15 additional minutes before slicing and serving. Cut small wedges and enjoy warm, at room temperature, or even chilled.

POMEGRANATE PECAN PIE

Makes 10–12 Servings

Pomegranates sure do get a lot of praise for their antioxidant rankings and supposed super powers, so why don't more people consider them when dessert rolls around? Perhaps it's an image problem—in this case, they're being sold as too healthy for their own good. Don't forget that taste comes first, and those tiny arils can play in the pastry kitchen along with the best of them! Mixing pomegranate into the classic pecan pie yields a dessert that is greater than the sum of its parts. Traditionally super-sweet syrup is perfectly tempered by tangy pomegranate juice, and the seeds finish off each slice with a resounding crisp bite. Considering those purportedly healthy components, if you really want to, maybe you can reason that it makes for an adequately balanced breakfast, too.

1 Blind-Baked Wholesome Whole Wheat Crust (page 44) or Classic Crust (Page 36)
⅓ Cup Cornstarch
1 Cup Plain Non-Dairy Milk

½ Cup Pomegranate Molasses
½ Cup Amber Agave Nectar
½ Teaspoon Salt
6 Tablespoons Non-Dairy Margarine, Cut into Pieces

1 Teaspoon Vanilla Extract
1½ Cups Toasted Pecan Halves
To Finish:
⅓ Cup Fresh Pomegranate Arils

In a medium saucepan, vigorously whisk together the cornstarch and about half of the non-dairy milk, forming a loose slurry. Be sure to beat out any lumps of starch, especially those that might be sticking to the bottoms or sides of the pan, before stirring in the remainder of the "milk." Add the pomegranate molasses, agave, and salt to the pan before setting it over medium heat on the stove.

Continue stirring gently the whole time the heat is on, and soon enough you should see bubbles begin to break around the edges of the liquid. Start whisking a bit faster, until the mixture reaches a full boil. Immediately turn off the stove and whisk in the margarine and vanilla, allowing the residual heat to melt the margarine. Finally, add the pecans.

Quickly transfer the filling into your baked and cooled crust, using a spatula to further distribute the nuts if they seem to have all landed in one spot. Sprinkle the pomegranate arils evenly across the top of the filling, and gently press them in with your fingers.

Let cool completely, waiting at least a full hour and a half, before serving.

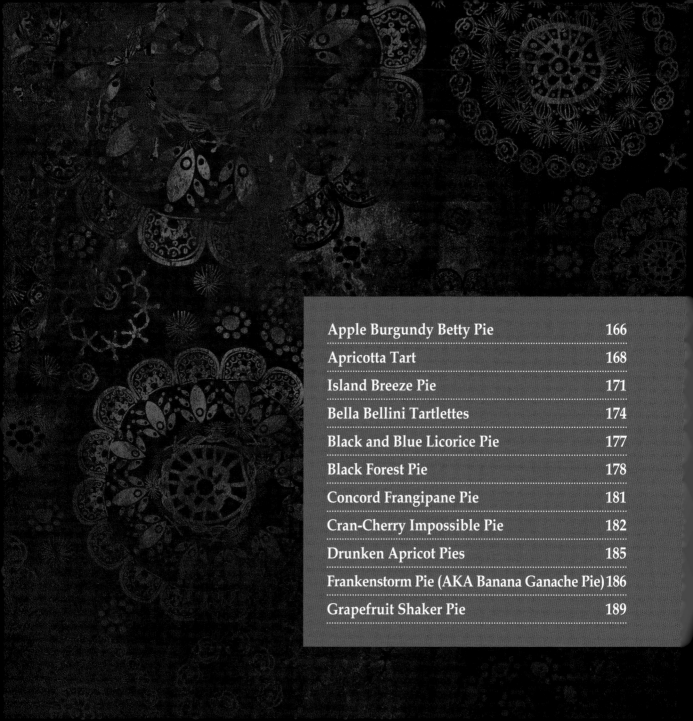

FRUIT PIES

APPLE BURGUNDY BETTY PIE

Make 8–10 Servings

Crisps, crumbles, and cobblers fight each other for distinction, all too often simply lumped together. Each fruit dessert differs in the topping; the contrast of crunchy oatmeal, streusel, or biscuit dough makes a world of difference. Moreover, the variations don't end there. The Brown Betty, one of the earliest American desserts, bears still another topping—sweetened breadcrumbs. Layered with apple slices, the crumbs create a slightly darker brown appearance than the others. It's time to make this permutation unmistakable; burgundy wine effectively kicks up both the flavor and color in one fell splash.

Bread Crumb Topping:
1½ Cups Panko Bread Crumbs
½ Cup Dark Brown Sugar, Firmly
  Packed
1 Tablespoon Natural Cocoa Powder
½ Teaspoon Lemon Zest
½ Teaspoon Ground Cinnamon
½ Teaspoon Ground Ginger
¼ Teaspoon Ground Cloves
⅛ Teaspoon Salt

5 Tablespoons Non-Dairy Margarine
  or Coconut Oil, Melted
Apple-Burgundy Filling:
3½–4 Cups (About 1½ Pounds)
  Peeled, Sliced, and Cored Sweet
  Red Apples
½ Cup All-Purpose Flour
2 Tablespoons Whole Flaxseeds,
  Ground
¼ Cup Granulated Sugar

½ Teaspoon Baking Powder
1 Teaspoon Ground Cinnamon
⅛ Teaspoon Ground Nutmeg
¼ Teaspoon Salt
¾ Cup Burgundy Wine
1 Tablespoon Lemon Juice
1 Tablespoon Olive Oil

Preheat your oven to 350 degrees and lightly grease a 9-inch pie plate.

Prepare the crumb topping first, so that it's ready to go when you are. Stir together the bread crumbs, sugar, cocoa, lemon zest, spices, and salt in a medium bowl. Break up the sugar and make sure that the spices are well distributed before proceeding. Drizzle in the melted margarine or coconut oil, stirring to moisten all of the bread crumbs. Don't worry that the mixture doesn't clump together; it should be very loose and coarse.

In a large bowl, stir together the flour, ground flaxseeds, sugar, baking powder, spices, and salt. Add in the apple slices and toss gently to coat. Mix the wine, lemon juice, and oil together in a separate bowl before pouring them into the large bowl as well. Stir to incorporate, until there are no more dry patches of flour remaining.

Scatter about ¼ cup of the crumb mixture evenly over the bottom of the greased pie pan. Gently pour the apple mixture on top, being careful not to disturb the crumbs, and smooth the filling into a flat layer. Sprinkle the remaining crumbs all over the top before sliding the pie into the oven.

Bake for 40–45 minutes until the crumbs are browned and a toothpick inserted into center comes out clean but moist. Cool for at least 15 minutes before serving.

APRICOTTA TART

Makes 8–10
Servings

This pie was born of nothing more than a silly typo. Sloppy keyboarding led to the invention of the word "apricotta," which seemed so fitting to describe a dainty dessert composed of both apricots and vegan ricotta that it needed to be made into a reality. Never could I have imagined just how perfectly those tender stone fruits would pair with a lightly sweetened, slightly tart ricotta cream filling. My poor keyboarding skills turned out to be a blessing in this case!

1 Unbaked Vanilla Cookie Crust
(page 48), or Rawesome Fruit and
Nut Crust (page 49)

Poached Apricots:
1½ Cups Water
⅓ Cup Limoncello or Other Lemon
Liqueur
½ Cup Granulated Sugar
Zest of 1 Orange
¼ Cup Roughly Chopped Fresh
Lemongrass

1 Whole Vanilla Bean
1 Pound (6–8 Large) Firm but Ripe
Apricots, Halved and Pitted

Sweet "Ricotta" Filling:
½ Cup Raw Cashews, Soaked for 4–6
Hours
1 12-Ounce Aseptic Package Extra-
Firm Silken Tofu
2 Tablespoons Lemon Juice
2 Teaspoons Apple Cider Vinegar
3 Tablespoons Olive Oil

½ Cup Vanilla Vegan Yogurt
2 Teaspoons Nutritional Yeast
½ Teaspoon Salt
⅛ Teaspoon Ground Nutmeg
⅓ Cup Granulated Sugar

To Finish:
¼ Cup Shelled and Toasted
Pistachios
Vegan Honey-Flavored Syrup (page
73) or Grade B Maple Syrup

Preheat your oven to 325 degrees.

To poach the apricots, first combine the water, limoncello, sugar, orange zest, and lemongrass in a small saucepan. Slice the vanilla bean in half and use the side of the knife's blade to scrape out the sticky seeds inside. Add them into the pan, but reserve the pod for vanilla sugar (page 34) or another recipe. Set over medium heat and bring to a boil, simmering for 5 minutes to dissolve the sugar. Gently add in the apricot halves, lower the heat to medium-low, and cook for 5–8 minutes, until tender. Remove the pan from the heat, allowing apricots to sit in the syrup for 3 or 4 minutes before removing and letting them cool to room temperature on a separate plate. Peel away the skins if they come off easily, and if desired.

For the ricotta, thoroughly drain the cashews and the tofu of any excess liquid, to prevent the filling from becoming too watery. Toss them into your blender or food processor, along with all of the remaining ingredients for the filling. Pulse

Continued on page 170.

to combine, pausing to scrape down the sides of the bowl as necessary. Continue blending until mostly smooth; a little bit of texture is fine in this case.

Pour the filling into your waiting crust, smoothing it out evenly across the bottom. Retrieve your poached apricots, drain once more to prevent them from weeping later, and fit them around the pan as snuggly as possible, cut sides facing down. You may have one or two that can't quite squeeze in, but they're quite delicious eaten all by themselves, or fancied up with a scoop of ice cream.

Slide the tart into the oven and bake for 35–45 minutes, until the edges of the filling appear dry and set. Cool to room temperature before serving, but if you can wait, it tastes even better when thoroughly chilled. Drizzle liberally with "honey" or maple syrup and garnish with a sprinkle of whole pistachios over the top.

Save that flavorful poaching syrup and turn it into a delectable dessert topping! Remove the lemongrass before setting the pan back on the stove and allow the liquid to slowly reduce. Simmering gently over medium-low heat, it may take 45–60 minutes to thicken adequately and reduce down to a mere ½ cup. Your patience will be rewarded with an exquisite sweet elixir unlike any other.

ISLAND BREEZE PIE

Makes 8–12 Servings

If it were possible to wrap up a tiny taste of paradise in a crisp and flaky crust, I have a feeling it would go something like this: Sweet, juicy cubes of papaya intermingling with roasted macadamia nuts, set off by the sharpness of ginger, lime, and a surprising pinch of pepper. Even if the islands are hundreds or even thousands of miles away, one bite can provide the experience, albeit fleeting, in an instant.

2 Unbaked Classic Crusts (page 36)

Papaya Filling:

4½ Cups (1½ Pounds) Diced Fresh Papaya*

⅔ Cup Granulated Sugar

¼ Cup Cornstarch

Zest of 1 Lime

⅛ Teaspoon Black Pepper

2 Teaspoons Finely Grated Fresh Ginger

⅔ Cup Roasted, Roughly Chopped Macadamia Nuts

1 Tablespoon Coconut Oil, Melted

To Finish:

Golden Pastry Glaze (page 25)

Preheat your oven to 375 degrees.

Place the diced papaya in a large bowl and toss with the sugar, cornstarch, lime zest, and pepper to coat. Add the grated ginger and spread it throughout the pieces of fruit as evenly as possible, breaking up any large clumps. Introduce the macadamia nuts last, stirring gently to distribute. Transfer the filling to your lined pie pan, gently easing the chunks into an even layer across the bottom. Drizzle the melted coconut oil all over.

Roll out the second unbaked crust and cut it into ½-inch wide strips to make a lattice top if desired, or keep the sheet of dough whole to make a plain, vented upper crust. Gently apply the upper crust to the top of your filled pie and crimp the edges. Lightly brush the upper crust with golden pastry glaze before sliding the pie into the oven.

Bake for 20 minutes at 375 degrees, and then reduce the heat to 350 degrees. Bake for an additional 35–45 minutes longer, until the crust is brown and the juices begin to bubble through the lattice or vents. If the edges brown too fast, cover them with strips of aluminum foil or a pie shield about halfway through baking. Cool for at least 30 minutes before serving.

Continued on page 173.

Papayas can vary immensely in size, sweetness, and even color! There are actually two types of papayas, which explains this vast discrepancy. Hawaiian papayas are smaller and pear-shaped, but the greatest difference is that the flesh is far sweeter and more flavorful. Mexican papayas are oblong fruits that are very large, weighting an average of 4–5 pounds each. I much prefer the Hawaii varieties, naturally, but the trouble is finding a reputable source. More than half of the papayas imported from the islands are GMO, which was a necessary last resort to prevent the fragile fruit from being overcome by the once-prevalent papaya ring virus. If you object to these modified crops, seek out only the following non-GMO varieties: Solo/Kapoho Solo, Tainung No. 1, Mexican Red/Mexican Yellow, or Orange Queen.

*To cut a papaya into neat little cubes, first slice the fruit in half, from pole to pole. Scoop out the black seeds inside and discard or save for another recipe. (They taste peppery and make an excellent addition to basic vinaigrette.) Working on one half at a time, score the flesh into squares, then run your blade from the top to bottom of the piece, as closely to the skin as possible, freeing the cubes from the peel. Discard the peel and repeat with the second half.

BELLA BELLINI TARTLETTES

Makes 10–12 Servings

Celebrations call for champagne, and not just for drinking. Blend peach puree into sparkling wine and you have yourself a Bellini, which is worth celebrating in and of itself. Rather than confining the intoxicating combination to skinny flutes, set it free inside tiny tart shells, each one far more satisfying that a mere sip. Though the effervescence bubbles out during baking, you can add a pinch of unflavored popping candy right before serving for an entirely new sort of zip and fizz.

1 Unbaked and Unrolled Classic
  Crust (page 36)
Peach Bellini Filling:
1½ Pounds (About 4 Medium) Very
  Ripe Peaches
2 Teaspoons Lemon Juice

1 Tablespoon Cornstarch
1 Cup Dry Sparkling White Wine
  (Such as Prosecco) or Champagne
¼ Cup Granulated Sugar
½ Whole Vanilla Bean

To Finish:
Unflavored Popping Candy*
  (Optional)

Pit the peaches and chop the flesh roughly before placing it in your blender or food processor. Add in the lemon juice, cornstarch, champagne, and sugar. Pulse to incorporate and then thoroughly puree. Allow 4–5 minutes for the skin to break down and become blended; pass through a fine mesh strainer if necessary, to achieve a perfectly smooth puree.

Transfer the puree to a medium-size saucepan and set over moderate heat. Split the vanilla bean in half and use the side of your knife blade to scrape out the sticky seeds. Add them into the saucepan and reserve the spent pod for making vanilla sugar (page 34) or another recipe. Bring to a boil and then reduce heat, to keep the mixture at a steady simmer. Cook for 20 minutes to thicken, then let cool completely.

Preheat your oven to 375 degrees.

Roll out your dough on a lightly floured surface to ⅛ inch thick. Use a round 4½-inch cookie cutter to punch out circles. Gather up the scraps, re-roll the dough, and repeat until you have 12 circles. Ease the circles into 4-inch round metal tartlette molds, pressing them into the corners and smoothly up the sides. Set all the molds on a flat baking sheet for easier maneuvering later. Alternatively, cut 4-inch round circles and ease them into 12 standard muffin pans.

Pour the cooled bellini filling almost up to the top of each tart shell. If desired, cut fun shapes out of any excess dough to embellish the tops. Simply lay the additional dough gently on top of the puree so that it doesn't sink.

Bake for 24–28 minutes, until the crust is golden. Let cool completely and chill for at least 2 hours before serving. Top with popping candy at the very last minute, if desired.

*Popping candy, also known as Pop Rocks®, fizz and pop when mixed with water, or in the case of this dessert, when placed on the tongue. The candies packaged in single servings are usually found in fruity flavors, but unflavored carbonated crystals can be found anywhere stocking "molecular gastronomy" ingredients, or online at Willpowder.com. The crystals are very sensitive to heat and moisture; store extras in an airtight container in a cool place to ensure that they don't lose their crackle.

BLACK AND BLUE LICORICE PIE

Makes 8–12 Servings

Easily the most polarizing flavor in the confectionery universe, there are no two ways about licorice; you either adore that fennel-like zest or you'd rather drink cough syrup for dessert. While it may be impossible to show those staunchly anti-licorice campaigners the light, careful pairing could easily win over some new fans. Picking up the mellow notes of blackberries and blueberries, licorice gains greater depth, tempering the harsh bite that drives many away. As the candies soften in the oven, they take on a texture eerily similar to the fruits themselves, utterly transforming the licorice into something extraordinary.

2 Unbaked Classic Crusts (page 36), Wholesome Whole Wheat Crusts (page 44), or Rye Crusts (page 45)
¾ Cup Granulated Sugar
3 Tablespoons Cornstarch
½ Teaspoon Ground Cinnamon

¼ Teaspoon Salt
1 Heaping Cup (6 Ounces) Soft Licorice Candy
3 Cups (12 Ounces) Fresh Blueberries

2 Cups (10 Ounces) Fresh Blackberries
1 Teaspoon Apple Cider Vinegar
1 Tablespoon Olive Oil

Preheat your oven to 400 degrees.

In a large bowl, stir together the sugar, cornstarch, cinnamon, and salt to combine. Chop the licorice candy into berry-sized pieces and add it in, along with both types of berries, tossing to coat with the dry ingredients. Drizzle in the vinegar and oil last, stirring gently to incorporate without crushing the berries.

Pour the filling into your prepared pastry crust, distributing the candy and fruits as evenly as possible throughout.

On a lightly floured surface, roll out the second piece of dough to about ⅛ inch thick. Use cookie cutters of any shape or size your heart desires to punch out an ornamental topping to the pie. Lay the shapes on top of the berry filling so that it's only loosely covered, with plenty of negative space in between the dough pieces.

Move the pie into the oven, tent with aluminum foil, and immediately turn down the oven to 375 degrees. Bake for 40 minutes before removing the tent. Afterward, bake for an additional 20–25 more minutes, until golden brown.

BLACK FOREST PIE

Makes 8–12 Servings

Can't see the forest for the cherries? Take a step back, cut the cake out of the equation, and lose the layers. Cherries and chocolate bake together into a dark, devilish pie filling, offset by the lightness of coconut whipped cream. Unburden the decadent German torte of all its fussy finishes for an even greater payoff in pie.

1 Unbaked Chocolate Pastry Crust (page 37) or Classic Crust (page 36)

Chocolate-Cherry Filling:
¾ Cup Granulated Sugar
¼ Cup Cornstarch

¼ Cup Dutch-Processed Cocoa Powder
¼ Teaspoon Salt
4 Cups (2½ Pounds) Fresh Sweet Cherries, Pitted and Stemmed
2 Tablespoons Lemon Juice

1 Cup (6 Ounces) Semi-Sweet Chocolate Chips
To Finish:
Coconut Whipped Cream (page 52)
15–20 Fresh Sweet Cherries

Preheat your oven to 375 degrees.

Stir together the sugar, cornstarch, cocoa, and salt in a large bowl, to thoroughly blend all of the dry goods. Add in the cherries, lemon juice, and chocolate chips, gently tossing to coat without crushing the fragile fruits. Spoon the filling into your prepared pie crust, including any of the excess dry ingredients that didn't manage to adhere to the cherries. It will come in handy for soaking up all of the fruit juices later, so just pile it all on top.

Bake the pie for 20 minutes, then reduce the temperature to 350. Don't open the door, and bake the pie for 35 minutes longer, or until the filling is bubbly and the crust looks dry and crisp. Let the pie cool for at least 25 minutes before digging in. If you'd like to garnish it as photographed, let cool completely before piping a border of whipped coconut cream all the way around the edge and topping the rosettes with fresh cherries.

CONCORD FRANGIPANE PIE

*Makes 8–12
Servings*

Becoming an adult leads to more mature tastes suitable for a well-developed palate, leaving many childhood pleasures behind. No longer do the one-note, sweet-or-savory, unchallenging flavors appeal in quite the same way. Some foods, however, defy all laws of time and space, finding a spot in our stomachs from infancy to old age. Peanut butter and jelly sandwiches are a perfect example, finding fans so enthusiastic that restaurants serving only PB&J really do exist.

If you do find yourself craving the comfort of that timeless nutty sandwich, leave the white bread for child's play. Frangipane may sound fancy, but it's really just a custardy almond filling, closely linked to the creamy peanut spread of sandwiches past. Factor in a few fresh concord grapes, concentrating their jammy sweetness with a trip to the oven, and just like that, that familiar old favorite is all grown up.

1 Unbaked Classic Crust (page 36) or
   Wholesome Whole Wheat Crust
   (page 44)

Almond Frangipane:
¼ Cup Creamy Almond Butter

¼ Cup Non-Dairy Margarine
½ Cup Granulated Sugar
¼ Cup Unsweetened Applesauce
½ Teaspoon Almond Extract
1 Cup Almond Meal

1 Tablespoon Arrowroot
¼ Teaspoon Salt
1 Pound Seedless Concord Grapes*

Preheat your oven to 375 degrees. In the bowl of your stand mixer, cream together the margarine, almond butter, and sugar with the paddle attachment until homogeneous, light, and fluffy, similar to the consistency of frosting. Add the applesauce and almond extract, mixing to incorporate. Scrape down the sides of the bowl as needed before adding the almond meal, arrowroot, and salt. Stir at low speed until thoroughly combined.

Use a wide spatula to fold half of the grapes into the frangipane. The mixture will be fairly thick, so be careful not to crush the grapes. Transfer the filling into your unbaked pie shell, smoothing it out evenly across the bottom. Sprinkle the remaining grapes over the top, gently pressing them into the batter.

Move the pie into the oven and tent with aluminum foil after the first 30 minutes of baking, to prevent the crust from burning. Bake for a total of 40–50 minutes, until the frangipane is just beginning to brown and is set around the edges. Let cool completely before serving.

*Due to high demand and low supply, seedless concord grapes can sometimes be tough to find, even during their prime growing season. Thompson grapes, or a hybrid of the two known as Thomcord grapes, would make a fine substitute.

CRAN-CHERRY IMPOSSIBLE PIE

Makes 8–10 Servings

A little bit tart, a little bit sweet, every bite of this pie is slightly different, but always delicious. Think that cranberries have a place only on the Thanksgiving table? That's quite all right; try swapping in fresh raspberries or blackberries instead.

1½ Cups Cranberries, Fresh or Frozen and Thawed
1½ Cups Pitted Sweet Cherries, Fresh or Frozen, Thawed, and Drained

½ Cup Slivered Toasted Almonds
¾ Cup Plain Non-Dairy Milk
1 Teaspoon Almond Extract
3 Tablespoons Non-Dairy Margarine or Coconut Oil, Melted

¼ Cup Cornstarch
1 Cup Granulated Sugar
½ Cup All-Purpose Flour
½ Teaspoon Baking Powder
¼ Teaspoon Salt

Preheat your oven to 350 degrees. Lightly grease and flour a 9-inch pie pan. Toss the cranberries, cherries, and slivered almonds together, and evenly distribute the mixture in your prepared pie pan. Set aside.

In a large bowl, whisk together the non-dairy milk, almond extract, melted margarine or coconut oil, cornstarch, sugar, flour, baking powder, and salt, until smooth. Pour the batter over the fruits and nuts in the pie pan. Don't worry if it looks like a mess at first, the cranberries will float to the top.

Bake for 50–60 minutes until a toothpick inserted into the center (of the batter only, not touching the fruits) comes out clean. Let cool for at least 1 hour before serving.

DRUNKEN APRICOT PIES

Makes 14–16 Servings

By the very few who have witnessed me imbibing, I've been told I'm a very cheap drunk; all it takes is a scant glass of champagne for all sense of balance and coordination to abandon me. That's why I can only imagine how utterly sloshed these tiny dried apricots must become on a whole cup and a half of wine! Though the most potent proportion of alcohol will dissipate by the time the mini pies make it to the table, these boozy treats are not for teetotalers.

1 Unbaked and Unrolled Classic
   Crust (page 36)

Drunken Apricots:
½ Pound Unsulfured Dried Apricots
¼ Cup Granulated Sugar

1½ Cups Dry White Wine
¼ Cup Orange Juice
3 1-Inch Strips Lemon Zest
⅛ Teaspoon Salt
1 Whole Vanilla Bean

To Finish:
Golden Pastry Glaze (page 25)

Place the apricots in a medium saucepan over moderate heat, along with the sugar, wine, orange juice, lemon zest, and salt. Split the vanilla bean in half lengthwise, and use the side of your knife blade to scrape out the moist seeds. Add them into the mixture as well, and reserve the spent vanilla pod for making vanilla sugar (page 34) or another use.

Once the mixture comes to a boil, reduce the heat and simmer gently, stirring every five minutes or so, until the liquid is almost completely absorbed into the fruit. This should take about 25–30 minutes. Turn off the heat and let rest for about 20 minutes, until cool enough to handle. Transfer the stewed apricots to the bowl of your food processor, and pulse 4–5 times. You want the apricots to be very roughly chopped, not pureed.

Preheat your oven to 375 degrees and line two baking sheets with parchment paper or silpats.

Roll out the dough on a lightly floured surface to about ⅛ inch thick. Using a 3-inch round cookie cutter, punch out as many rounds as possible from the sheet of dough. Gather, re-roll the scraps, and repeat as necessary. You should end up with about 24–28 circles.

Arrange half the circles on the prepared baking sheet, spaced approximately 1 inch apart, and place about 2 tablespoons of filling in the center of each. Run a lightly moistened finger all the way around the border of each, and lay a second round of dough on top. Use the tines of a fork to seal and crimp the edges together. Use a very sharp knife to make a few slits in the top for venting. Repeat on the remaining mini pies.

Brush the top of each pie lightly with the golden pastry glaze, and then bake one sheet at a time, for approximately 22–27 minutes each. When golden brown all over, transfer the pies to a cooling rack and let rest for at least 15 minutes before eating. To store for later, let cool completely before sealing in an airtight container at room temperature for up to 5 days.

FRANKENSTORM PIE (AKA BANANA GANACHE PIE)

Makes 8–10
Servings

In the aftermath of Hurricane Sandy, our house lost power for a gut-wrenching seven days and nights, as temperatures dipped below freezing. Near the end of the week, when the darkness and cold became too much to bear, we sought shelter with our incredibly generous, hospitable extended family a few towns away. Easily the best outcome of a bad situation, things certainly felt far less desperate when wrapped in a cloak of central heating, bright lights, and wifi. There aren't words enough to express just how grateful I am that they would unhesitatingly take us all in. Instead of fumbling through awkward and insufficient "thank you's," it was best to manifest that sentiment into something edible, of course.

Dangerously ripe bananas sitting on the counter were the catalyst, and the pie was further fleshed out by available ingredients and the need for low-impact prep work in an unfamiliar kitchen. Bananas and chocolate, uncomplicated and unfussy; there would have been no recipe or record if not for the rave reviews. Silky ganache brightened by fruity accents and a tiny pinch of sea salt to finish, it seemed unremarkable at first, but now will never be forgotten.

1 Blind-Baked Graham Cracker Crust (page 42)

Banana Ganache Filling:
4 Medium-Size Ripe Bananas
3 Tablespoons Light Agave Nectar

1 Teaspoon Vanilla Extract
2 Tablespoons Non-Dairy Margarine
2 Cups (12 Ounces) Semi-Sweet Chocolate Chips

¼ Cup Vanilla or Plain Non-Dairy Milk

To Finish:
Coarse Sea Salt

For the filling, toss the peeled bananas into the food processor or blender and thoroughly puree, along with the agave and vanilla. Meanwhile, place the margarine, chocolate chips, and non-dairy milk in a microwave-safe dish and heat for about 1 minute. Stir well to smooth out the mixture and allow any remaining chips to fully melt. Reheat at intervals of 20 seconds if necessary, stirring well after each one.

Transfer the melted chocolate into the blender or food processor, and puree once more to fully integrate. Scrape down the sides of the bowl if necessary, to ensure that everything is incorporated. Once completely smooth, pour the filling into your prepared crust, smooth out the top, and sprinkle very lightly with a pinch of coarse sea salt.

Refrigerate for at least 3 hours before serving, or until set.

GRAPEFRUIT SHAKER PIE

Makes 8–12 Servings

Waste not, want not; nothing goes to waste when making a shaker pie. Lemons are the most common citrus of choice, but I much prefer to give the grapefruit some love, highlighting its bittersweet, invigorating flavor. To combat the mouth-puckering tartness inherent in the peels, this pie does need the full measure of sugar, no matter how astounding it may sound. Just cut yourself small slices and luxuriate in each intense, unrestrained, yet soothingly sweet grapefruit bite.

2 Unbaked Classic Crusts, 1 Unrolled
  (page 36)

Pink Grapefruit Filling:
1 Large Pink Grapefruit
2 Cups Granulated Sugar
¼ Teaspoon Salt
⅓ Cup Garbanzo Bean Flour
⅓ Cup All-Purpose Flour
3 Tablespoons Non-Dairy Margarine
  or Coconut Oil, Melted

To Finish:
Golden Pastry Glaze (page 25)
1–2 Tablespoons Turbinado Sugar
  (Optional)

Preheat your oven to 375 degrees.

Thoroughly wash and dry the grapefruit, since you're going to be eating the whole thing, rind and all. Using a mandoline or extremely sharp knife, slice the fruit paper-thin. The slices should be about .75–1 mm, and don't worry if the pieces aren't perfect rounds; a few odd shreds are fine too. Remove and discard seeds as you go. Cut the slices into quarters and place them in a large bowl. Add the sugar, salt, and both flours, tossing to coat.

Spoon the grapefruit mixture into your dough-lined pie pan, fitting the pieces into as even and tight a layer as possible. Drizzle the melted margarine or coconut oil all over.

Roll out the second round of dough on a lightly floured surface to ⅛ inch thick, to make the top crust. Make sure it's at least 2 inches larger in diameter than the pie pan itself, and carefully drape it over the filling. Trim crust as needed, leaving a 1-inch overhang. Fold and roll the excess under the bottom crust, pressing the edge to seal it, and crimp decoratively as desired. Brush the top lightly with golden pastry glaze, and sprinkle with turbinado sugar, if using.

Cut a few slits with a sharp knife to create steam vents, before baking for 20 minutes. Without opening the oven door, reduce the temperature to 350 degrees. Bake the pie for an additional 30–40 minutes from that point, or until the crust is golden brown all over. Let the pie cool for at least 30 minutes and serve it warm or at room temperature.

KILLER APPLE PIE

Makes 8–12 Servings

Before green juices flowed like water through the swift current of popular culture, there was still considerable trepidation over imbibing what looked like murky pond water. Rightly so, especially when wheatgrass, an old nemesis of many health-seekers, was blended into the mix. It was an effort to ease myself into the movement until I stumbled upon a rave-worthy juice haven in NYC. Visiting for the first time on a punishingly cold winter evening, the rare inclusion of one hot juice was a merciful find. Though the name sounds intimidating, "The Killer XX" was pure comfort from first sip. Green apples, lemon, ginger, and cayenne were the only ingredients, and yet the taste spoke of depth and balance. Realizing that it was almost like a tart, spicy apple pie in a glass, I hurried home and set about solidifying the concept.

2 Unbaked Classic Crusts (page 36), 1 Unrolled

Spicy Apple Filling:

3 Pounds (9–10 Medium) Tart Green Apples, Peeled, Cored, and Sliced

1 Tablespoon Lemon Juice

1–1½ Inches Fresh Ginger, Finely Grated (About 1 Tablespoon)

1 Cup Granulated Sugar

5 Tablespoons Cornstarch, Divided

Zest of 2 Lemons

¼ Teaspoon Cayenne Pepper

To Finish:

Golden Pastry Glaze (page 25)

Preheat your oven to 425 degrees.

After peeling, coring, and slicing all the apples, place them in a large bowl and quickly toss them with lemon juice, to prevent browning. Add the grated ginger and spread it throughout the pieces of fruit as evenly as possible, breaking up any large clumps. In a separate bowl, combine the sugar, 4 tablespoons of the cornstarch, lemon zest, and cayenne in a large bowl. Add the dry goods to the apples, mixing gently to incorporate.

Sprinkle the remaining tablespoon of cornstarch over the bottom of your unbaked pie crust. Spoon the sugared and spiced apples on top, fitting the pieces together as tightly as possible. Mound the apples up towards the center of the pan.

Roll out the second piece of dough on a lightly floured surface to ⅛ inch thick. Use a small cookie cutter to cut out a decorative window vent if desired, or simply use a sharp knife to cut a few vents in the center. Gently drape the dough over the hill of apples, and trim so that there's still about ¾-inch of dough overhanging the edge. Fold and roll the excess under the bottom crust, pressing the edge to seal it, and crimp decoratively as desired. Brush lightly with golden pastry glaze all over.

Tent with aluminum foil and bake for 15 minutes. Without opening the oven door, reduce the temperature to 375 degrees, and continue baking for 30 more minutes. Uncover the pie so that it can brown, and bake for a final 25–35 minutes after doing so. Let cool for at least 20 minutes before digging in; best served warm.

MA'AMOUL PIE

Ma'amoul cookies are such festive edibles that it's only fitting to find them frequently during holidays and other joyous times all across the Middle East. Many different types can be found, varying by the region and particular baker, but most are semolina shortbreads filled with either dates or nuts. Pressed into patterned molds, the textures that remain in the surface of the dough are equally unique, although the simple concentric circle is a common option. Sweetened entirely by dates, my pie adaptation skews the ratios in favor of that sticky, earthy filling, which is really the best part.

2 Unbaked Semolina Crusts (page 39), Cornmeal Crusts (page 38), or Classic Crusts (page 36), 1 Unrolled

Date Filling:
1 Pound Medjool Dates, Pitted
1 Cup Unsweetened Applesauce
1 Tablespoon Orange Blossom Water

½ Teaspoon Ground Cinnamon
½ Teaspoon Salt
To Finish:
Confectioner's Sugar (Optional)

Preheat your oven to 375 degrees.

Place the pitted dates, applesauce, orange blossom water, cinnamon, and salt in the bowl of your food processor, and pulse to combine. Pulse repeatedly to turn the mixture into a thick paste, but don't completely puree. It should still retain a bit of texture. Smooth the paste into your pastry-lined pie pan, leveling it off into an even layer.

Roll out the second round of dough on a lightly floured surface to ⅛ inch thick and about 12 inches in diameter, to make the top crust.

To achieve the pattern of concentric circles on top, the easiest method is to take a circular wire cooling rack and gently press it into the surface of the dough, leaving a shallow indentation from the wires. Alternatively, you can use the rim of variously sized glasses and bowls, starting with the smallest one in the center and working your way out to the largest one for the outermost ring. Cut a few discrete vents along these rings, evenly spaced and far enough apart that the design won't tear. Very carefully transfer the upper crust to the filled pie. Trim as needed, leaving a 1-inch overhang. Fold and roll the excess under the bottom crust, pressing the edge to seal it, and crimp the edges simply so as not to detract from the central pattern.

Bake for 35–40 minutes, until golden brown all over. Let cool completely before slicing and serving; store and serve at room temperature.

MAHALAPEÑO PIE

Makes 8–12 Servings

When pineapple and jalapeño meet, sweet and spicy fireworks will fly. Inspired by tropical adventures abroad, the secret ingredient is not one that can be bought or found in any store—the spirit of *mahalo* (the deepest sort of gratitude) is almost tangible when baked with care. It's a perfect sort of welcoming or thank you gift, especially since pineapples are a universal symbol of hospitality.

2 Unbaked Classic Crusts (page 36) or Cornmeal Crusts (page 38), 1 Unrolled

Pineapple-Jalapeño Filling:
½ Cup Granulated Sugar

3 Tablespoons Cornstarch
6 Cups (2⅓ Pounds) Diced Fresh Pineapple (About 1 Medium Pineapple)*
2 Tablespoons Lime Juice

½–1 Fresh Jalapeño, Seeded and Finely Minced
¼ Teaspoon Salt

To Finish:
Golden Pastry Glaze (page 25)

Preheat your oven to 400 degrees.

Toss together all the ingredients for the filling, adding more or less jalapeño to taste. Pour the pineapple mixture into your pastry-lined pie pan, distributing the pieces into an even layer.

Roll out the top crust on a lightly floured surface to about ⅛ inch thick and 11–12 inches in diameter. Gently drape the dough over the top of the pie and trim if needed, leaving a 1-inch overhang. Fold and roll the excess under the bottom crust, pressing the edge to seal it, and crimp decoratively as desired. Use a very sharp knife to cut 1-inch vents in the top, and lightly brush the exposed surface all over with golden pastry glaze.

After placing the pie in the oven, immediately reduce the heat to 350 degrees. Bake for 45 minutes, until the upper crust is evenly browned. Let cool for at least 30 minutes before serving. This pie is also delicious served chilled on a hot summer's day.

*Pineapple might look intimidating to break down, but it's really a softie with a tough exterior. Start by cutting off the leafy top and bottom so that the fruit is just a cylinder. Place the fruit on one of the flat ends and use your knife to slice away the outer peel, using a downwards sawing motion. Go back around and remove the "eyes" by cutting small "v" shaped grooves diagonally down either side of the eyes, working all the way around the fruit. Quarter the pineapple lengthwise, remove the woody core at the center, and finally dice the remaining flesh into neat little cubes.

MEMBRILLO PIE

*Makes 8–12
Servings*

Quince doesn't get a whole lot of love in the USA, if you can even find it at all, which is really a shame. It takes just a bit of coaxing to unleash the most incredible floral apple flavor from those once hard fruits, melting into a buttery jam over the stove. Membrillo is the ultimate expression of the quince, pureed and cooked down for so long that the sugars caramelize and the flavors intensify to entirely new heights. That sweetness makes it the perfect contrast to a more savory cheese plate, or in this case, a lightly salted cream cheese topping.

1 Unbaked Classic Crust (page 36) or
    Cornmeal Crust (page 38)
Quince Paste:
1½ Pounds (About 3 Medium) Ripe
    Quinces, Peeled, Cored, and
    Chopped

¼ Cup Lemon Juice
1 Cup Granulated Sugar
Cream Cheese Topping:
1 8-Ounce Container Vegan Cream
    Cheese
2 Tablespoons Cornstarch

1 Tablespoon Lemon Juice
¼ Teaspoon Salt

A traditional quince paste is perfectly smooth, much like a pâtes de fruits (AKA jelly candy), but this pie is much more interesting with a bit of texture to the filling, so I like to make my membrillo chunky. To accomplish that, take only two of the prepared quinces, along with the lemon juice, and thoroughly puree in your blender or food processor. Once completely smooth and similar to thick applesauce in consistency, transfer to a medium saucepan along with the remaining chopped quince and the sugar. Stir well and set over moderate heat.

Bring the mixture up to a boil and then reduce the heat to low. Be patient, because the process of cooking out the water and caramelizing the sugars takes a good deal of slow and steady cooking. Simmer very gently for 1½–2 hours, stirring occasionally and scraping the bottom and sides of the pan to make sure that nothing sticks, until the membrillo is thick and a deep rosy-pink hue. The cooking time can vary greatly depending on the size of your saucepan, since those with large bottoms have a greater cooking surface that can cook the mixture faster. If attempting to speed up the process with a bigger vessel, just be cautious and stir often to make sure the paste doesn't burn.

Turn off the stove and let cool for 15 minutes before transferring the warm quince paste to your prepared pie pan. Preheat your oven to 375 degrees.

The cream cheese topping comes together instantly, by comparison. Simply beat the "cream cheese," cornstarch, lemon juice, and salt together in your stand mixer with the paddle attachment, or in a large bowl with a wide spatula and a good bit of muscle. Once homogeneous, smooth the mixture over the quince paste in an even layer. If desired, use small cookie cutters to punch out simple shapes from leftover scraps of pie dough to decorate the top.

Bake for 35–40 minutes, until the pastry is lightly browned and the cream cheese layer appears set around the edges. Let cool completely before slicing. Enjoy either at room temperature or chilled.

PEAR PRALINE PIE

Makes 8–12 Servings

Comfort is the smell of pears baking in the oven, redolent of warming spices and brown sugar. One whiff and any worries about looming deadlines, challenging projects, or difficult days are instantly forgotten. If only someone could figure out how to bottle that scent, we might be well on our way to an effective anti-anxiety tonic. Until then, there's just no substitute for the real thing. Tucked into a blanket of pecan praline streusel, even the pears must feel cozy.

1 Unbaked Classic Crust (page 36) or
    Wholesome Whole Wheat Crust
    (page 44)

Spiced Pears:
3 Pounds (About 6 Cups; 5 Medium)
    Firm D'anjou or Bosc Pears,
    Peeled and Sliced
½ Cup Granulated Sugar

¼ Cup Cornstarch
2 Tablespoons Arrowroot
½ Teaspoon Salt
¾ Teaspoon Ground Cinnamon
¼ Teaspoon Ground Nutmeg
⅛ Teaspoon Ground Cardamom
Zest of ½ Lemon

Pecan Praline Topping:
½ Cup Dark Brown Sugar, Firmly
    Packed
½ Cup All-Purpose Flour
½ Cup Chopped Raw Pecans
¼ Teaspoon Salt
¼ Cup Non-Dairy Margarine, Melted

Preheat your oven to 400 degrees.

Place your sliced pears in a large bowl along with the sugar, cornstarch, salt, and spice. Toss gently to evenly distribute the dry goods and coat the fruits. Add the lemon zest last, and stir briefly to incorporate. Transfer the spiced pears to your pastry-lined pie pan and arrange the pear pieces in as even a layer as possible, packing them into the bottom tightly.

The praline topping is made just like your average streusel; combine the brown sugar, flour, pecans, and salt in a medium bowl, mixing lightly. Drizzle the melted margarine in on top and stir until the mixture is fully moistened and sticking together in coarse clumps. Sprinkle it all over the top of the pie. It may seem like a lot, but there really is room for all of it, and later you'll be happy you loaded it up!

Slide the pie into the oven and bake for 10 minutes. Without opening the oven, turn down the heat to 375 degrees and continue baking for 30 minutes more. If the edges of the crust appear to be browning too quickly, cover them with strips of aluminum foil halfway through the baking process. When finished, the fruit should be bubbly and the crust golden.

Let cool for at least 20 minutes before enjoying.

RHUBARB HEART PIES

Makes 10–12 Servings

Have a heart! These sweet little personal pies are made for lovers—rhubarb lovers, that is. Rather than covering up the uniquely tangy and tart flavor of those ruby red stalks with other fruits, it positively shines enhanced with only a bit of real vanilla bean.

1 Unbaked and Unrolled Classic
    Crust (page 36)
Vanilla Bean-Rhubarb Filling:
1 Pound Fresh Rhubarb, Cut into
    ½-Inch Lengths (About 3–3½
    Cups)

½ Cup Granulated Sugar
2 Tablespoons Cornstarch
½ Teaspoon Lemon Zest
2 Tablespoons Grade B Maple Syrup
1 Teaspoon Olive Oil
½ Whole Vanilla Bean

To Finish:
Golden Pastry Glaze (page 25)

Before you even think of turning on the oven, you'll want to prepare and chill the filling to give it proper time to thicken. Begin by combining the rhubarb, sugar, cornstarch, lemon zest, maple syrup, and olive oil in a medium saucepan over medium-low heat. It will be very dry at first, but resist the temptation to add liquid. Before you know it, the rhubarb will become very soft and juicy. Just be sure to keep stirring the mixture until the danger of the dry goods burning has passed. Split the vanilla bean lengthwise and use the side of your knife blade to scrape out the moist seeds within. Add them to the saucepan and stir well to incorporate. Reserve the spent pod for making vanilla sugar (page 34) or another use.

Cook the mixture until it begins to bubble. Reduce the heat to low, and let simmer gently, stirring occasionally, for 10–15 minutes. Remove from the heat and chill thoroughly (at least 1–2 hours) before using.

When the filling is good to go, preheat your oven to 375 degrees and line two baking sheets with parchment paper or silpats.

Roll out the dough to ⅛-inch thick on a lightly floured surface. Using a heart-shaped cookie cutter measuring about 3–3½ inches across the widest point, punch out as many hearts from that sheet of dough as possible. Gather up the scraps, re-roll, and repeat as necessary until all the dough is used. Take a second, smaller heart-shaped cookie cutter to remove a window of dough in the center of half of the larger hearts; these will become the top crusts.

Place the whole large hearts evenly spaced on your prepared baking sheet, no more than 6 pies per sheet. Spoon 1–2 tablespoons of filling in the centers, being careful not to go overboard, to prevent the excess from bubbling out when baking. Run a lightly dampened finger all the way around the edge of each heart, and gently lay one of the hearts with a cut-out center on top. Press the edges together with a fork to seal and crimp the dough at the same time. Brush the tops with golden pastry glaze and bake one sheet at a time.

Bake for 15–20 minutes, until the pies are golden brown all over. Transfer to a wire rack and cool for 10 minutes before eating, or completely before storing in an airtight container at room temperature.

ROASTED STRAWBERRY AND TOMATO GALETTE

Makes 6–8 Servings

Strawberries and tomatoes, though seemingly an odd couple, bring out the best in each other for both sweet and savory preparations. As comfortable together in a salad as in this free-form pie, the savory, gently acidic bite of the tomatoes accentuates the sweetness of the berries. Just like a pinch of salt can make any dessert pop, the combination of these apparently discordant tastes, in the right balance, creates a more complex and satisfying dish. I focused on featuring these key players and nothing else, further intensifying their basic flavors by first roasting them, concentrating their inherent sweetness and tartness, before baking the bright red jam in a flaky, sugar-sprinkled crust.

"Rustic" is one of my least favorite words in the English language, applied to everything from house decor to clothing, but especially to food. One might be tempted to describe the humble galette as such, but first consider all of the love and care that goes into each pastry. They may not be fancy, but every single element is keenly attended to, making sure they taste their absolute best. Simple needn't mean plain, dull, or forgettable. Especially when this unusual dessert is topped with finely shredded basil for the ultimate herbaceous finishing touch, it's hard to top it—except with a single scoop of creamy vanilla ice cream, perhaps.

1 Unbaked and Unrolled Classic
  Crust (page 36)
**Sweet Roasted Strawberries and
  Tomatoes**:
1 Pound (About 4 Cups)
  Strawberries, Hulled and Halved

10 Ounces (About 2 Cups) Cherry
  Tomatoes
1 Whole Vanilla Bean, Split and
  Scraped
½ Cup Granulated Sugar
2 Tablespoons Olive Oil
¼ Teaspoon Salt

Pinch Freshly Ground Black Pepper
To Finish:
Golden Pastry Glaze (page 25)
1–2 Tablespoons Turbinado Sugar
4–6 Leaves Fresh Basil, Thinly Sliced
  (Optional)

Preheat your oven to 350 degrees and pull out an 11 x 7-inch rectangular baking dish.

Toss together all of the ingredients for the filling, saving the vanilla bean pods for another application. (Best use: Make some vanilla sugar!) Spread the sugared fruits inside your baking dish, making sure that everything is in one even layer. Bake for 60–65 minutes, stirring every 15 minutes or so. After about 20 minutes, the mixture will become very

Continued on page 204.

juicy—don't panic, this is a good thing! Continue cooking until the excess liquid thickens, becoming syrupy, and the fruit is fairly jam-like in consistency. Cool completely before proceeding.

To complete the galette, roll out the unbaked pie crust on a lightly floured surface to a thickness of about ⅛ inch, as round as you can possibly make it. Don't fret if it's a bit misshapen; that will only add to the charm. Transfer the flat circle of crust to a silpat or parchment paper-lined baking sheet, and pile your jammy roasted strawberries and tomatoes in the center. Spread the filling out evenly in the middle, leaving a clean border of about 2 inches all around. Fold over the edges to contain the filling, and lightly brush the exposed crust with golden pastry glaze. Sprinkle lightly with turbinado sugar.

Bake in a preheated 350 degree oven for 30–40 minutes, until the crust is golden brown and the filling bubbly. Don't fret if some of the juices spill over the sides, as there will still be plenty within. Let cool for at least 15 minutes before topping with a light touch of fresh basil, if desired, and serve immediately while still warm.

MANGO CHUTNEY PIE

Makes 8–12
Servings

Blissfully unaware of most cuisines beyond standard American fare throughout my formative years, the exotic spices that make up Indian food were completely absent from my early life. That dearth of piquancy also explains the reluctance to accept chutney as a valid edible substance. At once arrestingly sour and sweet, it could be made of any combination of fruits or vegetables imaginable, each with their own subtle nuance, but the intensity always pulled my taste buds in violently different directions.

Now, with a more open mind and developed palate, I can finally appreciate the concept of balance that a properly prepared chutney can bring to a meal, complimenting the burn of a powerful curry or enlivening plain rice. Thus, although this dessert interpretation does skew more to the sweet side of the concept, it is delicious paired with a dollop of vanilla yogurt, rather than the standard scoop of ice cream.

Consider the royal icing ornamentation purely optional, a side project for those graced with patience and a steady hand. Dressed up for a fancy occasion in a stunning henna-inspired design, I must thank Cori Burke, of Indrani's Mehndi, from the bottom of my heart, for turning this particular pie into a work of edible art.

2 Unbaked Classic Crusts (page 36),
  1 Unrolled
Sweet Mango Chutney:
½ Cup Golden Raisins
¼ Cup Orange Juice
3 Small Green Apples, Peeled, Cored,
  and Diced (2½–3 Cups)
3 Medium-Size, Firm but Ripe
  Mangoes, Peeled, Pitted and
  Diced (3–4 Cups)

¼ Cup Finely Diced Crystallized
  Ginger
1 Cup Granulated Sugar
2 Tablespoons Cornstarch
1 Tablespoon Arrowroot
½ Teaspoon Ground Cinnamon
½ Teaspoon Ground Ginger
½ Teaspoon Salt
¼ Teaspoon Turmeric
¼ Teaspoon Cayenne Pepper

⅛ Teaspoon Ground Black Pepper
Chocolate Royal Icing (Optional):
2 Cups (½ Pound) Confectioner's
  Sugar
¼ Cup Natural Cocoa Powder
2 Tablespoons EnerG Egg Replacer
3–4 Tablespoons Water

Preheat your oven to 350 degrees.

First, place the raisins and orange juice in a microwave-safe container and heat for 60 seconds. Let sit and stir thoroughly. If the raisins haven't absorbed almost all of the liquid, heat once more for 15–45 seconds, pausing every 15 seconds to stir and make sure the fruits don't overheat.

Continued on page 207.

In a large bowl, toss together the prepared apples, mangoes, rehydrated raisins, and crystallized ginger. Stir gently to distribute the pieces of fruit evenly throughout the mixture.

In a separate bowl, whisk together the sugar, cornstarch, arrowroot, and all of the spices and seasonings. Once the dry mixture is homogeneous, add it into the bowl of fruit, and toss to coat. Pour the chutney filling into your crust-lined pan, distributing the pieces to form a fairly even layer.

Roll out the second round of dough on a lightly floured surface, to ⅛ inch thick, for the top crust. Make sure it's at least 2 inches larger in diameter than the pie pan itself, and carefully drape it over the filling. Trim as needed, leaving a 1-inch overhang. Fold and roll the excess under the bottom crust, pressing the edge to seal it, and crimp decoratively as desired. Cut a few slits with a sharp knife, to create steam vents.

Tent pie with a piece of aluminum foil and bake for 45 minutes. Uncover the pie at that point and return it to the oven, baking for an additional 15–25 minutes longer. Once the crust is evenly browned, remove it from the oven and let cool completely. Serve as is, or chill for 30 minutes before preparing the royal icing.

It helps if the pie is completely cool when applying the icing, for better adhesion. Once your pie is chilled, make the icing by combining the dry ingredients in your stand mixer first, and then slowly drizzling in the water, one tablespoon at a time, until the mixture reaches a pipable consistency. Err on the side of less liquid, because you can always add more, but you can't take it out. Transfer the icing to a piping bag fitted with a very small round tip, and apply your edible henna design as desired.

ROSEMARY-PEACH TARTE TATIN

Makes 8–10
Servings

By combining peaches and corn, two highlights of the season, this upside-down pie is my ode to summer. Simple, straightforward, and only fit for the freshest produce, I'd say it perfectly sums up the spirit of those warmer months.

1 Unbaked and Unrolled Cornmeal
   Crust (page 38)

2–3 Large (1 Pound) Firm but Ripe
   Peaches, Pitted and Sliced
½ Teaspoon Dried Rosemary

⅔ Cup Granulated Sugar
2 Tablespoons Lemon Juice
3 Tablespoons Non-Dairy Margarine

Preheat your oven to 375 degrees.

Lightly grease a 9-inch round pie pan and place the sliced peaches in the bottom, arranged in concentric circles. Overlap slightly if necessary so that they are fitted tightly together and cover the entire pan. Sprinkle the rosemary evenly over the peaches, and set aside.

Combine the sugar and lemon juice in a medium saucepan over moderate heat. Stir just until the sugar has dissolved, and then begin swirling the pan gently to keep the mixture moving. Let the mixture cook for 8–12 minutes until it caramelizes and turns amber brown.

Meanwhile, roll out your crust on a lightly floured surface to ⅛ inch thick. Cut out a 9½-inch diameter circle and place it near the pie pan.

When the caramel has reached a golden hue, immediately turn off the heat and add the margarine. Stir slowly, allowing the residual heat to fully melt the margarine, and then pour the hot caramel all over the sliced peaches. Ease the large circle of pastry over the top, and move the whole thing into the oven.

Bake for 40–50 minutes, until the pastry is golden and the caramel is bubbling up over the edges.

Remove from oven and let cool for 15 minutes. Don't wait any longer or the caramel will being to harden and your tarte tatin may become stuck inside the pan. Place a serving dish right on top of the pie pan and quickly but carefully invert it, so that the peaches are facing up and the whole assemblage has been released from its vessel.

Serve warm, with vanilla ice cream on the side if desired.

Thyme-Apricot Tarte Tatin: Just like it sounds, all you need to do is swap equal measures of rosemary for thyme and peaches for apricots to make this alternative flavor combination.

STRAWBERRY CEREAL STREUSEL PIE

Makes 8–12 Servings

Give your breakfast a boost! Don't resign yourself to a bowlful of plain, dry cereal when you could use it as a vehicle for a generous helping of plump and juicy strawberries. The cornflake base is somewhat more fragile than your average pastry, but that crumbly, crispy quality makes it all the more enjoyable to eat.

Cornflake Crust and Streusel:
6½ Cups Cornflake Cereal, Divided
½ Cup All-Purpose Flour
½ Cup Granulated Sugar
¼ Teaspoon Ground Cinnamon
¼ Teaspoon Salt

½ Cup Non-Dairy Margarine, Melted
¼ Cup Chopped Raw Walnuts
Strawberry Filling:
3 Pounds Fresh Strawberries, Hulled
  and Quartered (8–9 Cups)
¾ Cup Granulated Sugar, Divided

¼ Cup Cornstarch
Zest of 1 Lemon
½ Teaspoon Vanilla Extract

Toss together the prepared berries and ¼ cup of the sugar and let macerate at room temperature for 30 minutes. Drain off the excess liquid, to prevent the filling from becoming watery. Add the remaining sugar, cornstarch, lemon zest, and vanilla, tossing gently to combine.

Meanwhile, preheat your oven to 350 degrees and lightly grease a 9-inch springform pan.

Place 5½ cups of the cornflakes, flour, sugar, cinnamon, and salt into your food processor and pulverize into a fine flour. Pulse the margarine into the powder to incorporate, and measure out 3 cups of the mixture. Press this portion into the bottom of your springform pan and about an inch up the sides.

Bake for 15 minutes and let cool.

Combine the leftover cereal mixture with the remaining cornflakes and walnuts to form the streusel; set aside.

Spoon the strawberry filling into the baked cereal crust, and top with the cornflake streusel. There will be a lot of the topping, so don't be afraid to really pile it on.

Tent with aluminum foil and bake 30 minutes. Uncover and bake for an additional 25–30 minutes, until golden and bubbling. Let cool completely before serving.

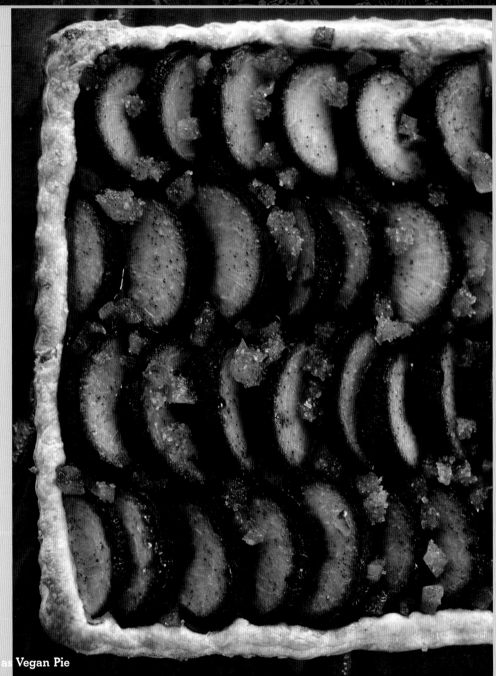

SUGARED PLUM TART

Makes 10–12 Servings

You would be hard pressed to find a more elegant last-minute dessert. Plums kissed with a bit of heat become so juicy they practically explode, concentrating their natural sweetness into a jammy consistency. Boldly spiced, chewy chunks of ginger kick the flavor up into brave new territory. It's a dessert easy enough for anyone to make, and tasty enough for everyone to enjoy.

1 Sheet Frozen Puff Pastry, Thawed
1½ Pounds (About 5 Medium) Fresh
    Plums, Pitted and Sliced

1 Tablespoon Olive Oil
¼ Teaspoon Ground Cloves
⅛ Teaspoon Ground Allspice

3 Tablespoons Finely Minced
    Crystallized Ginger
3 Tablespoons Turbinado Sugar

Preheat your oven to 400 degrees and line a baking sheet with a piece of parchment paper or a silpat.

On a lightly floured surface, unfold and roll out the sheet of puff pastry into a large rectangle approximately ⅛ inch thick. Carefully transfer it to your prepared baking sheet. Take a very sharp paring knife and score a border all the way around the dough, a little less than half an inch from each edge. Prick the interior rectangle repeatedly, at about 1-inch intervals, to allow steam to vent while the tart is baking.

In a large bowl, toss together the sliced plums, oil, dry spices, and crystallized ginger. Stir to evenly coat the fruit. Arrange the plums in even lines, slightly overlapping, across the center of puff pastry, keeping the borders clear. Try to distribute the ginger evenly so that there's a good amount in each bite.

Sprinkle the turbinado sugar over the whole tart before sliding it into the oven. Bake for 20 minutes, until the plums are fork-tender and the pastry is golden brown all over. Let cool for at least 10 minutes before enjoying.

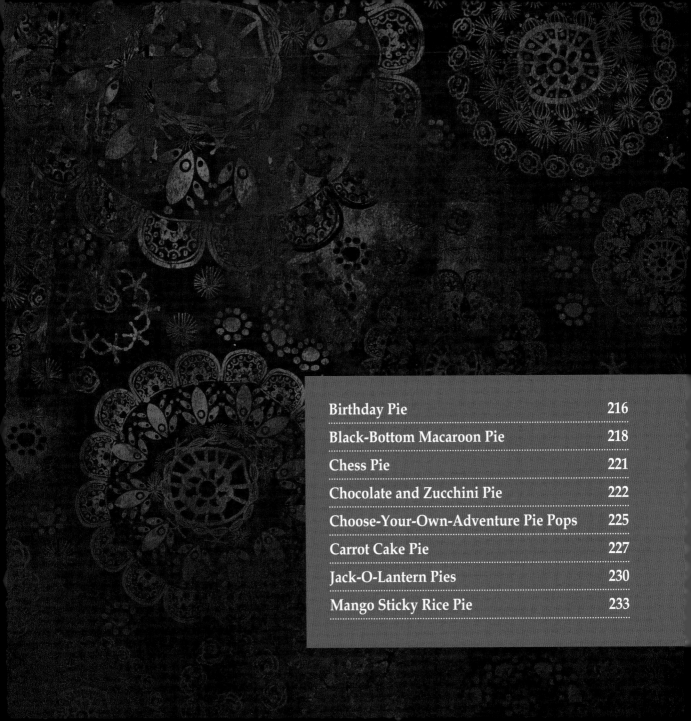

WILD CARD PIES

BIRTHDAY PIE

Makes 8–12
Servings

The never-ending battle of pie versus cake has claimed countless otherwise intelligent, peaceful souls. An excellent case can be made for each, an even match on almost all counts, but then someone always has to bring up birthday parties. "There can't be a birthday without a cake!" the cake provocateurs inevitably cry. To that, I respond with the solution to end all arguments, once and for all: the birthday pie. Not merely a crusted concoction to be served on one's birthday, but a pie that in fact tastes like white birthday cake, complete with rainbow sprinkles. I'm not picking sides here, but I think just one bite could win the war.

1 Unbaked Classic Crust (page 36) or
   Chocolate Pastry Crust (page 37)
Confetti Cake Batter:
1¾ Cups Cake Flour
1 Cup Confectioner's Sugar
¾ Teaspoon Baking Powder
½ Teaspoon Salt
6 Tablespoons Non-Dairy Margarine,
   Melted

1 6-Ounce Container Vanilla Vegan
   Yogurt
½ Cup Plain Non-Dairy Milk
½ Teaspoon Apple Cider Vinegar
2 Teaspoons Vanilla Extract
¼ Cup Rainbow Sprinkles
Fluffy Vanilla Frosting:
½ Cup Non-Dairy Margarine
1½ Cups Confectioner's Sugar

½–1½ Tablespoons Plain Non-Dairy
   Milk
½ Teaspoon Vanilla Extract
Pinch Salt
To Finish:
Additional Rainbow Sprinkles

Preheat your oven to 350 degrees.

Sift the cake flour, confectioner's sugar, baking powder, and salt into a large bowl. In a separate bowl, whisk together the melted margarine, yogurt, non-dairy milk, vinegar, and vanilla, stirring until smooth. Pour the liquid ingredients into the bowl of dry, and use a wide spatula to bring the two together. Stir just until there are no pockets of flour remaining, but be careful not to over-mix; a few lumps are just fine.

Quickly stir in the sprinkles, then immediately transfer the mixture into the unbaked pie shell. Don't let it sit around too long at this point, as the colors from the sprinkles may begin to run.

Bake for 25–30 minutes, until a toothpick inserted into the center pulls out cleanly. Let cool completely before frosting. To make the frosting, toss the margarine into the bowl of your stand mixer and beat thoroughly, until softened. Add in the confectioner's sugar and mix on a low speed, so as not to spray the powder everywhere. Once the sugar is mostly incorporated, pause to scrape down the sides of the bowl with your spatula before increasing the speed. Add in the non-dairy milk, vanilla, and salt, and whip on high for 5 minutes or so, until the frosting is smooth and fluffy.

Transfer to a piping bag and pipe a decorative border around the edge of the pie, or spoon dollops on individual slices. Finish with an additional pinch of sprinkles on top.

BLACK-BOTTOM MACAROON PIE

Makes 8–12 Servings

Passover was the only time I saw macaroons paraded out when I was younger, being one of the few sweet treats available without flour. Always "fresh" out of the can but tasting long past expiration, there was good reason why they never made any other appearances throughout the year. The only redeeming aspect would be if they were dipped in chocolate, because then the cocoa coating could be carefully nibbled away, leaving the unpalatable haystacks behind. Distasteful childhood desserts behind me, this pie makes up for lost time. Moist, tender, and tasting of real, full-bodied coconut, not a crumb will be left behind.

Cocoa-Coconut Crust:

2⅓ Cups Unsweetened Shredded Coconut

3 Tablespoons Potato Starch or Cornstarch

1 Tablespoon Granulated Sugar

¼ Cup Dutch-Processed Cocoa Powder

6 Tablespoons Non-Dairy Margarine or Coconut Oil, Melted

6 Ounces (1 Cup) Semi-Sweet Chocolate Chips

1½ Teaspoons Olive Oil

Coconut Macaroon Filling:

½ Cup Plain Mashed Potato (From 1 Peeled, Steamed, Cooled, and Pureed White Potato)

¼ Cup Coconut Oil, Melted

½ Cup Canned Full-Fat Coconut Milk

2 Tablespoons Potato Starch or Cornstarch

1¼ Cups Granulated Sugar

1½ Teaspoons Vanilla Extract

½ Teaspoon Salt

2½ Cups Unsweetened Shredded Coconut

Preheat your oven to 325 degrees and lightly grease a 9-inch round pie pan.

To make the coconut crust, break out your food processor and toss in the coconut. Sprinkle the starch and cocoa on top and then drizzle the melted margarine over. Pulse to combine and break the coconut down into smaller pieces, but you don't want to completely puree it. Once the mixture is crumbly but mostly cohesive, dump it out into your pie pan and use your fingers to press it evenly up the sides and along the bottom. Bake for 10–12 minutes and let cool, but keep the oven on.

Place the chocolate chips and olive oil in a microwave-safe container. Heat on full power for 60 seconds, then stir thoroughly to melt the chips. If there are still solid pieces remaining, heat for an addition 30–45 seconds, pausing every 15 seconds or so to stir, until the mixture is silky smooth. Pour into the baked coconut crust and spread evenly across the bottom and up the sides. The goal is to coat the interior as evenly as possible. Let chill in the freezer for 10 minutes, or until the chocolate as solidified.

For the filling, beat together the mashed potato, melted coconut oil, coconut milk, starch, sugar, vanilla, and salt until smooth and homogeneous. Stir in the shredded coconut last, mixing with a wide spatula to incorporate into the mixture. Transfer to your prepared crust and smooth out the top.

Bake for 45–55 minutes. Tent with foil after 30 minutes if the edges of the filling seem to be browning too quickly. When finished, the pie filling should be golden-brown around the edges and lightly set in the center, with a very slight wobble when tapped. Cool completely before slicing and serving.

For a Passover-appropriate pie, opt for the potato starch instead of cornstarch, and coconut oil instead of margarine.

CHESS PIE

*Makes 8–12
Servings*

I wish I could claim to know the origins of chess pie, or even a plausible theory, but I really haven't the slightest clue. It seems that no one can agree where it came from or why it was so named, but the basic contents are invariably the same: Flour, butter, eggs, and a whole lot of sugar. That is, until now. Utilizing the unlikely secret ingredient of potato to replace the bulk and stability of eggs, with a few tricky flavor boosters thrown in such as kala namak, it tastes uncannily of the classic custard. Scaling back considerably on the sweetness also helps the character of this revitalized pie to shine through.

1 Unbaked Classic Crust (page 36)
  Or Wholesome Whole Wheat
  Crust (page 44)
½ Cup Non-Dairy Margarine
1½ Cups Granulated Sugar

2 Teaspoons Vanilla Extract
3 Cups Fluffy Riced Yukon Gold
  Potatoes* (About 12–13 Ounces)
2 Tablespoons All-Purpose Flour
¼ Cup Plain Non-Dairy Milk

½ Teaspoon Black Salt (Kala Namak)
¼ Teaspoon Turmeric (Optional, for
  Color)

Preheat your oven to 375 degrees.

In the bowl of your stand mixer, thoroughly cream together the margarine and sugar until homogeneous. Scrape down the sides of the bowl with your spatula and add in the vanilla. Beat once more to incorporate. Introduce the prepared and cooled potatoes next, along with the flour, "milk," kala namak, and turmeric. Mix on low speed just until smooth. Be careful not to overdo it, or else you'll end up turning the starch from the potatoes into a gluey, sticky mess.

Pour the golden batter into your prepared pie crust, smoothing it evenly across the bottom and leveling the top as needed. Bake for 55–60 minutes, until the edges are firm and a toothpick inserted into the center pulls out cleanly. Let cool completely before serving. This pie is delicious both at room temperature and chilled!

*To prepare your potatoes properly, start by peeling about a pound. Place them in a medium pot with cool water, and bring it to a boil. Turn down the heat so that the water stays at a constant simmer, and cook until the potatoes are fork-tender. Drain and let them dry for about 5 minutes. Press them through a potato ricer or food mill, and measure the volume of the potatoes unpacked. Bear in mind that a more accurate measurement can be obtained by weight.

CHOCOLATE AND ZUCCHINI PIE

Makes 8–12 Servings

If chocolate and zucchini make such a winsome couple in quick breads, why shouldn't they be allowed to shine in other baked goods? Blending seamlessly into this cocoa-drenched filling, that green summer squash could be honestly mistaken for apple slices. Go ahead, try serving your friends a slice and see if anyone can guess its vegetative secret.

2 Unbaked Classic Crusts (page 36) or Chocolate Pastry Crusts (page 37), 1 Unrolled

2½ Pounds Zucchini, Peeled, Cut Lengthwise, and Sliced into ¼-Inch Thick Half-Moons (6–7 Cups)

½ Teaspoon Salt

½ Cup Granulated Sugar

½ Cup Dark Brown Sugar, Firmly Packed

½ Teaspoon Ground Cinnamon

1½ Teaspoons Cream of Tartar

1 Tablespoon Cornstarch

2 Tablespoons Natural Cocoa Powder

1 Teaspoon Apple Cider Vinegar

⅔ Cup (4 Ounces) Semi-Sweet Chocolate Chips

2 Tablespoons Non-Dairy Margarine or Coconut Oil

To Finish:

Golden Pastry Glaze (page 25)

½–1 Teaspoon Granulated Sugar

Preheat your oven to 400 degrees.

Before we get to any of the sweet stuff, first toss the sliced zucchini with salt, then let sit 30 minutes to extract some of the water within. Blot away excess liquid with a paper towel and you're good to go.

In a large bowl, mix together both sugars, cinnamon, cream of tartar, cornstarch, and cocoa. Add in the zucchini, vinegar, and chocolate chips, tossing to evenly coat. Don't worry if there are dry ingredients at the bottom of the bowl that don't stick to the squash; those are still necessary for soaking up the additional water expressed by the zucchini once baked.

Spoon the filling into the prepared crust, distributing the zucchini throughout the pan as evenly as possible. Drizzle the melted margarine or coconut oil over the top before covering with a vented upper crust. Crimp the edges and brush the top crust lightly with golden pastry glaze before sprinkling with sugar.

Cover with an aluminum foil tent before sliding the pie into the oven. Bake for 20 minutes at 400, and then reduce the heat to 375 without opening the door. Bake for an additional 30–40 minutes, uncovering in the last 15 minutes to evenly brown. Let cool for at least 20 minutes before serving.

Zucchini Mock Apple Pie: Omit cocoa and chocolate chips, add 1 tablespoon cornstarch. Increase the cinnamon to 2 teaspoons and add ½ teaspoon ground allspice and ¼ teaspoon nutmeg.

Pegan Pie

CHOOSE-YOUR-OWN-ADVENTURE PIE POPS

Makes 9–10
Pies Per Filling
Recipe

As a dessert meant for sharing, pie is typically reserved for special occasions, and rarely made on a whim. Pie *pops*, however, are individual portions of pie, perfect for any day and any taste. Not to mention, nearly everything is tastier if it comes on a stick. The sky's the limit for flavorful fillings—consider any jams, preserves, or jellies in the fridge fair game—but look to the following recipes for more adventurous ideas.

Chocolate Mousse Filling:
6 Ounces (½ Aseptic Package) Extra-
    Firm Silken Tofu
½ Teaspoon Vanilla Extract

Pinch Salt
1 Cup (6 Ounces) Semi-Sweet
    Chocolate Chips

2 Tablespoons Light Corn Syrup or
    Light Agave Nectar
2 Tablespoons Non-Dairy Margarine

Drain away any excess water from the tofu before tossing it into your food processor and giving it a whirl. Add in the vanilla and salt, and blend just enough to break it down and get it mostly smooth. Set aside.

Place the chocolate chips, syrup, and margarine in a microwave-safe container, and heat on full power for 60 seconds. Let sit 30 seconds, and then stir thoroughly until smooth. If the chips haven't all entirely melted, continue to microwave at intervals of 30 seconds, stirring well after each time.

Pour the melted chocolate into your food processor with the tofu, and puree. Pause to scrape down the sides periodically, until everything has been incorporated and the chocolate mousse is silky-smooth. Let rest for 20–30 minutes to cool slightly, but do not chill before using in your pie pops.

Maple-Pecan Filling:
¼ Cup Grade B Maple Syrup
¼ Cup Plain Non-Dairy Milk

Pinch Salt
1 Tablespoon Cornstarch

¾ Cup Roughly Chopped, Toasted
    Pecans
½ Teaspoon Vanilla Extract

In a medium saucepan over medium-low heat, vigorously whisk together the maple syrup, non-dairy milk, salt, and cornstarch, so that there are no lumps of starch remaining. Cook until the mixture comes up to a lively bubble, whisking constantly so that nothing sticks or burns. Once fully boiling and significantly thickened, turn off the heat and stir in the pecan pieces and vanilla. Cool completely before baking into pie pops.

Poached Pear Filling and Dipping Sauce:

¾ Cup Red Wine

¼ Cup Apple Cider or Apple Juice

⅓ Cup Granulated Sugar

Zest of 1 Orange, Finely Grated

1 Teaspoon Ground Cinnamon

2 Firm but Ripe Bosc or D'Anjou Pears, Peeled, Cored and Diced

1 Tablespoon Lemon Juice

2 Tablespoons Cornstarch

Set a medium saucepan over moderate heat on the stove, and combine the wine, apple cider, sugar, orange zest, and cinnamon. Bring the mixture up to a gentle simmer, making sure that the sugar has completely dissolved, before proceeding.

Prep the pears and immediately toss them with lemon juice, to prevent browning. Add half of the diced pear pieces into the saucepan and allow them to poach for 10 minutes. After that time has elapsed, introduce the remaining pear to the mixture as well. This will ensure that there's a good mixture of softer and firmer pieces of pear once baked. Let it cook for 5 minutes longer, and then turn off the heat and drain the wine away from the pear pieces, reserving both.

Return the spiced wine to the pot, and bring the heat back to medium. Simmer until syrupy and reduced by ½ or ¾ depending on how thick you want your dipping sauce to be; about 30–45 minutes. Cool and chill until ready to serve.

Meanwhile, cool the pear pieces completely and chill for at least 30 minutes. Water will likely continue to condense and escape from the fruit, so be sure to drain the excess liquid again. Toss with the cornstarch, and your filling is ready to go.

For Assembly (Per Each Filling Recipe):

1 Unbaked and Unrolled Classic Crust (page 36)

9–10 Lollipop or Popsicle Sticks

Golden Pastry Glaze (page 25)

Turbinado Sugar (Optional)

Preheat your oven to 375 degrees and line a baking sheet with parchment paper or a silpat. Set aside.

On a lightly floured surface, roll out the dough to a thickness of about ⅛ inch. Use a round cookie cutter about 2 ½ inches in diameter to punch out matching circles. Gather up excess pie dough and re-roll to get more circles out of it. Move half of them over to your prepared baking sheet, and place a lollipop stick across each center, near the top of the shape. Spoon 1½–2 teaspoons of filling mounded directly in the center, on top of the stick. To get consistent amounts of filling, it helps to use a small, 25mm cookie scoop.

Brush the edges of the exposed pie dough around the filling with non-dairy milk. Take one of the remaining plain circles and with your hands, gently stretch the top crust out so that it's slightly larger than the bottom, to accommodate the mound of filling. Lay it on top, and carefully press around the edges, keeping the filling contained. Crimp the edges firmly with a fork, and poke once in the very center to vent. Brush with golden pastry glaze all over and lightly sprinkle turbinado sugar evenly on top.

Bake pies for 15–20 minutes until golden brown. Let rest on the sheet for 10 minutes before transferring to a cooling rack.

CARROT CAKE PIE

Makes 8–12 Servings

Everyone knows that carrot cake is practically health food, making that second slice completely justified. You're only getting in your an extra serving of vegetables, after all! It's a shame that most recipes throw in just a few token shreds of the orange roots, blowing a hole right through that weak excuse. On the other hand, this pie rendition manages to fit a full pound and a half of carrots into one little pastry crust, really emphasizing their natural sweetness and earthy flavor. Nutritionally speaking, it still won't take the place of a salad, but you can't exactly top a salad with cream cheese frosting.

1 Unbaked Classic Crust (page 36) or Wholesome Whole Wheat Crust (page 44)

Roasted Carrot Puree:
1½ Pounds Carrots, Peeled
1 Tablespoon Olive Oil

Carrot Cake Batter:
1 Cup Plain Non-Dairy Milk
¼ Cup Non-Dairy Margarine or Coconut Oil, Melted

1 Cup Dark Brown Sugar, Firmly Packed
1 Teaspoon Vanilla Extract
1¾ Teaspoons Ground Cinnamon
¾ Teaspoon Ground Ginger
¼ Teaspoon Baking Powder
¼ Teaspoon Salt
¼ Cup Garbanzo Bean Flour
½ Cup Raisins

¼ Cup Chopped and Lightly Toasted Walnuts (Optional)

Cream Cheese Frosting:
1 8-Ounce Package Vegan Cream Cheese
¼ Cup Non-Dairy Margarine
1 Cup Confectioner's Sugar
½ Teaspoon Vanilla Extract

Preheat your oven to 400 degrees and line a baking sheet with a silpat or aluminum foil.

You can't make carrot cake without the carrots, which is why this one begins with a smooth carrot puree. Peel your carrots and chop them into 1½–2 inch pieces, halving them lengthwise if they're particularly thick. The specific measurement isn't particularly important, but getting pieces approximately the same size is. This will ensure that they all cook at about the same rate, without burning smaller chunks or undercooking larger ones. Toss with oil to coat and spread them out in one even layer on your prepared baking sheet. Roast for approximately 30 minutes, until lightly browned around the edges and fork-tender.

Cool for at least 15 minutes before smoothly pureeing in your food processor or blender. Transfer to a large bowl which can accommodate the rest of the filling ingredients.

Reduce the oven temperature to 350 degrees.

Introduce the non-dairy milk, melted margarine or coconut oil, brown sugar, vanilla, spices, baking powder, and salt to the carrot puree in that very same large bowl. Stir well until smooth and homogeneous. Toss the chickpea flour, raisins,

and walnuts (if using) together separately before adding them into the big bowl as well. Mix to distribute the goodies equally throughout the thick batter and stir out any dry patches of flour.

Pour the carrot batter into your prepared pie crust and bake for 45–50 minutes, until the filling is firm around the edges but still slightly jiggly in the center, much like a cheesecake. Cool completely before moving the pie into the fridge to chill. Allow at least 2 hours before frosting and slicing.

Make the frosting by simply beating together the cream cheese and margarine in your stand mixer until smooth, adding in the sugar and vanilla, and then whipping on high speed for a minute or two, until homogeneous, light, and creamy. Apply to the border of your pie as desired.

JACK-O-LANTERN PIES

*Makes 4
Servings*

After the ghouls and goblins have gone home, candy plundered and devoured, the remnants of Halloween can be seen strewn around town for days to come. It's not just the toilet paper thrown by mischief-makers causing all the mess—jack-o-lanterns grow limp with age, and animals begin to gnaw their own designs out of the once wicked smiles. A good squash is a terrible thing to waste! Rescue those pumpkins before it's too late and repurpose them into something truly delicious. The flesh of smaller gourds tends to be sweeter, but pumpkins of all shapes and sizes are edible. Just make sure they're thoroughly cleaned and have no paint or ink marks.

1 Unbaked and Unrolled Classic
   Crust (page 36) or 1 Sheet Frozen
   Puff Pastry, Thawed
Roasted Pumpkin:
4 Cups Peeled and Diced Sugar
   Pumpkin or Kabocha* (About ½

of a Medium-Sized, 3.5-Pound
   Winter Squash)
2 Tablespoons Olive Oil
¼ Teaspoon Salt
Spiced Custard:
¾ Cup Plain Non-Dairy Milk

¼ Cup Granulated Sugar
¼ Cup Dark Brown Sugar, Firmly
   Packed
1 Tablespoon Cornstarch
1 Teaspoon Five-Spice Powder
   (page 12)

Preheat your oven to 400 degrees and line a baking sheet with a piece of parchment paper or aluminum foil.

Toss the cubed pumpkin or kabocha with the oil and salt to coat. Spread the pieces out in an even layer on the prepared baking sheet, and bake for 25–30 minutes, until fork-tender and lightly browned around the edges. After removing the sheet from the oven, reduce the heat to 375 degrees.

Meanwhile, in a medium saucepan over moderate heat, vigorously whisk together the non-dairy milk, both sugars, cornstarch, and five-spice, being sure to beat out any lumps of starch. Whisk occasionally as the mixture comes up to temperature, until it reaches a rolling boil. Immediately remove the pan from the heat.

Set four 4-ounce ramekins on a baking sheet for easier transport in and out of the oven. Distribute the roasted squash between the cups, and then pour equal amounts of the cooked custard into each as well.

On a lightly floured surface, roll out the pastry to about ⅛ inch thick. Cut out four rounds slightly larger than the tops of your ramekins, and carve out pumpkin faces for the vents. Carefully move the top crusts onto the ramekins, centering them over the filling.

Bake for 20–25 minutes, until the pastry is golden brown. Let cool for at least 15 minutes before enjoying.

*Even a small gourd can be a giant pain to prepare. Many methods will lead you to the same results, but what works best for me is breaking down my pumpkin one piece at a time. You'll need a very sharp, very sturdy knife for this job, as well as a strong peeler (ceramic blades or flimsy metal are sure to snap). Take your knife and wedge it into the center of the pumpkin with as much force as you can safely muster. Split it in half, and then pause to scrape out the innards with a spoon. Save the seeds to roast later—they're one of my favorite fall snacks! Once cleaned, cut each of the halves in half again (yielding 4 pieces total) and then cut those pieces into thirds (making 12 wedges). Peel each piece, then chop those wedges into ½-inch cubes.

Bananas Vegan Pie

MANGO STICKY RICE PIE

Makes 8–12 Servings

Thailand doesn't have nearly the same sort of dessert culture as European countries, but that's not to say that there's not a sweet tooth to be found. Rather, sugary snacks are more common than after dinner treats. A bounty of exotic fruits is always close at hand, so many of those more traditional treats put them to good use. In this case, juicy mango tops off coconut-infused sticky rice to create *Khao Neeo Mamuang*, otherwise known simply as mango sticky rice. Using the rice itself as a shell to contain the sauce-like pudding and tender fruit slices turns it into a family-style treat, perfect for sharing.

Sticky Rice Crust and Coconut Pudding:

1½ Cups Water
1 Cup Sushi Rice
1 14-Ounce Can Full-Fat Coconut Milk, Divided

¾ Cup Granulated Sugar, Divided
¼ Teaspoon Salt
¾ Cup Plain Non-Dairy Milk
3 Tablespoons Cornstarch
1 Tablespoon Coconut Oil
1 Teaspoon Vanilla Extract

To Finish:

1–2 Ripe Mangoes, Peeled, Pitted, and Thinly Sliced
1 Tablespoon Toasted Sesame Seeds

This pie is made entirely on the stovetop, so there's no need to preheat the oven this time! Pour the water into a medium saucepan over high heat and bring it to a rolling boil. Add in the rice, stir once, reduce the heat all the way down to low, and cover. Cook gently for 14–16 minutes, until the grains are tender and have absorbed all of the water. Turn off the heat but keep covered for 5 minutes longer.

Stir ½ cup of the coconut milk, ¼ cup of the sugar, and all of the salt into cooked rice while still hot. Let stand, covered, for 20 minutes or until rice absorbs all the liquid and is cool enough to handle. Press the coconut rice into the bottom and up sides of a lightly greased 9-inch pie plate. Move the crust into your fridge to chill while you prepare the filling.

Place the remaining coconut milk and sugar, along with the non-dairy milk and cornstarch, into a medium saucepan. Whisk thoroughly to beat out any potential lumps before turning on the heat to medium. Cook, stirring periodically, until the liquid has significantly thickened and comes up to a full boil. Turn off the heat and stir in the coconut oil and vanilla to incorporate. Let cool for 10 minutes before proceeding.

Retrieve the crust and pour the pudding into the center. Smooth it out to the edges before tucking it back into the fridge. Let cool completely to allow it to set; at least 2 hours.

Right before serving, arrange sliced mangoes in a circular fan pattern in the center and sprinkle liberally with sesame seeds.

MAPLE SHOO-FLY PIE

Makes 8–12 Servings

Having a "wet bottom" would ordinarily sound like a terrible affliction, but in the case of shoo fly pie, it's the very best part. Sticky, gooey, and delightfully messy, this classic Amish treat is typically flooded with dark molasses. Bread crumbs lend some stability to the syrupy pastry and are shrewdly thrifty, too. As a die-hard lover of all things maple, this seemed like the perfect opportunity for a syrup swap out. Rather than topping it off with stale bread, I decided to up the ante a bit with brown sugar crumbs fit for the most buttery coffee cake.

1 Unbaked Classic Crust (page 36), Chocolate Pastry Crust (page 37), or Wholesome Whole Wheat Crust (page 44)

Crumbs:
1 Cup All-Purpose Flour
⅓ Cup Dark Brown Sugar, Firmly Packed
2 Tablespoons Non-Dairy Margarine, Melted
¼ Teaspoon Salt

Maple Filling:
¾ Cup Boiling Water
¾ Teaspoon Baking Soda
¾ Cup Grade B Maple Syrup
2 Tablespoons Whole Flaxseeds, Ground
¼ Cup Unsweetened Applesauce
1 Teaspoon Vanilla Extract

Preheat your oven to 400 degrees.

For the crumbs, place the flour, brown sugar, melted margarine, and salt in a small bowl and stir with a fork until the mixture forms very loose, dry crumbs. Set aside.

The filling begins with a very old-fashioned first step that involves dissolving the baking soda in the hot water. Stir the two together in a large bowl before whisking in the maple syrup, ground flaxseeds, applesauce, and vanilla. Once homogeneous, turn your attention back to the crumbs. Reserve ½ cup of the crumb mixture, and stir the rest into the bowl of liquid ingredients. Stir just to moisten and incorporate.

Scatter half (¼ cup) of the reserved crumbs over the bottom of the unbaked pie shell. Pour the filling on top and sprinkle the remaining crumbs evenly over the surface. Carefully slide the pie into your oven, since the filling is fairly loose and could slosh out if you're not gentle.

Bake at 400 degrees for 10 minutes, then reduce heat to 350 degrees and bake for an additional 20–25 more minutes. You'll know it's done when the filling puffs up, begins to look dry on top and starts to crack slightly. Don't panic if the center falls slightly as it cools; that just means you've made it correctly! Let cool completely before slicing.

MARGARITA JELLY SHOT TARTLETTES

Makes 18–24 Servings

Let loose and live the pie life with a few intoxicating crusted jelly shots! More than just a vehicle for getting happily tipsy, these potent mini tarts sparkle with bright citrus flavor, only lightly sweetened to retain a strong bite. Make a bold statement by serving a plateful at your next party.

1 Unbaked and Unrolled Classic
Crust (page 36)
Margarita Jelly Shots:
6 Tablespoons Tequila

6 Tablespoons Water
¼ Cup Lime Juice
2 Tablespoons Triple Sec
1 Tablespoon Light Agave Nectar

1 Teaspoon Agar Powder
To Finish:
Coarse Sea Salt

Preheat your oven to 350 degrees.

On a clean, lightly floured surface, roll out your dough to ⅛ inch thick. Use a 3-inch round cookie cutter to punch out circles, gathering up the scraps, re-rolling and repeating until all the dough is used. Ease each circle into a cup of a mini muffin tin. Trim away any excess dough and poke the bottoms once or twice with a fork to create steam vents. Place in the freezer for 15 minutes before baking.

Bake the empty crusts for 10–14 minutes, until golden brown. If any of them threaten to slide down the sides of the pan, immediately take a small spoon and press it gently along the sides while the dough is still warm and malleable. Let cool before filling.

After removing the blind-baked crusts from the oven, you can move on to preparing the jelly. Vigorously whisk together all of the margarita shot ingredients in a small saucepan. Stir out any clumps of agar before turning on the heat to medium-low, mixing all the while. Cook until the mixture comes up to a rolling boil and quickly turn off the heat. The longer you cook the filling, the less alcohol content will be in the final shot, so don't let it linger on the burner. Pour the liquid jelly into your waiting crusts, filling each almost to the top. Let rest, undisturbed, until solidified and cooled to room temperature.

Move the jelly shots into the fridge for at least 2–3 hours, until chilled. Sprinkle each one with a pinch of sea salt right before serving.

MATCHA MOCHI PIE

*Makes 8–12
Servings*

Leave mochi pounding to the experts. When casually attempted by the curious amateur, only pain and mushy rice can come of it. Old-school mochi is made from repeatedly smashing cooked sticky rice with a giant wooden hammer, but in my limited experience, a little shortcut yields much better results than starting from scratch. Finely ground mochiko guarantees a perfectly smooth filling, and takes the physical exertion out of the equation. Though the texture may turn some off, it's a nostalgic treat for anyone yearning for a taste of Japan.

1½ Cups Mochiko
1 Cup Granulated Sugar
1 Teaspoon Cornstarch
½ Teaspoon Baking Powder

⅛ Teaspoon Salt
1 Tablespoon Matcha Powder
1¾ Cup Plain Non-Dairy Milk
½ Cup Plain Vegan Yogurt

¼ Cup Non-Dairy Margarine or
   Coconut Oil, Melted
½ Teaspoon Vanilla Extract

Preheat your oven to 350 degrees and lightly grease a 9-inch round pie tin or tart pan.

The unique composition of this pie allows it to stand up all by itself as an "impossible pie," without a traditional rolled or pressed crust. Thus, you can dive right in and start mixing it up right away! In a large bowl, combine the mochiko, sugar, cornstarch, baking powder, and salt. Sift in the matcha, making sure that any clumps of powder are removed, as they're very difficult to smoothly incorporate after the fact. Stir well to distribute all of the dry goods equally throughout.

Separately, whisk together the non-dairy milk, yogurt, melted margarine or coconut oil, and vanilla. Once homogeneous, pour these liquids into the large bowl of dry ingredients. Whisk vigorously to combine, beating out all lumps of starch that may form. Go ahead and beat the tar out of it; there's no gluten so you can't over-mix. Get out your frustrations, get aggressive! Whisk mercilessly for 2–3 minutes.

Pour the batter into your prepared pan and bake for 45–50 minutes, until the edges are firm and the top is no longer shiny. Let cool completely before slicing and serving.

Do not refrigerate, as the cold makes it hard and unpleasant. Store at room temperature, covered with plastic wrap, for up to three days.

OLD-FASHIONED OATMEAL PIE

Having leftover slices of pie to eat for breakfast is one of the greatest pleasures of being an avid baker. Just knowing that something sweet awaits is enough to easily propel me out of bed, even at the earliest, most uncivilized hours. Some pies are more suitable than others for the most important meal of the day, though. One made of wholesome rolled oats is just the ticket, perfectly fit for morning revelry. An especially good ace to have up your sleeve when hosting overnight guests, simply bake the pie the night before and you'll be a rock star when breakfast time rolls around.

1 Unbaked Wholesome Whole Wheat Crust (page 44)

1 Cup Unsweetened Applesauce

¾ Cup Dark Brown Sugar, Firmly Packed

½ Cup Grade B Maple Syrup

6 Tablespoons Non-Dairy Margarine, Melted

1½ Teaspoons Vanilla Extract

1 Tablespoon Whole Flaxseeds, Ground

1½ Teaspoons Ground Cinnamon

½ Teaspoon Salt

1½ Cups Old-Fashioned Rolled Oats

½ Cup Chopped Walnuts

Preheat your oven to 350 degrees.

In a large bowl, combine the applesauce, brown sugar, maple syrup, melted margarine, vanilla, ground flaxseeds, cinnamon and salt. Stir in the oats and walnuts last, making sure they're thoroughly coated in the loose batter and evenly distributed throughout. Pour the mixture into your waiting crust and smooth out the top with your spatula.

Bake for 45 minutes or until set. The interior may still be slightly moist if using the toothpick test, which is exactly what you want. Let cool for at least 20 minutes before digging in. To elevate this pie to genuine dessert status (or for a super decadent breakfast), go ahead and throw a generous scoop of ice cream on top, too.

PUP TARTS

Makes 8–10 Servings

Every dog has their day, and every dog should have their own pie! Especially on my beloved pooch's birthday, it only seems right to give her something extra special to celebrate. If homemade personal pies meant just for your canine friend sounds a bit extreme, just think of it as an oversized dog treat with fruit filling.

1 Unbaked and Unrolled Wholesome Whole Wheat Crust (page 44)
1 Large Ripe Banana

⅓ Cup Unsweetened Applesauce
2 Tablespoons Creamy Peanut Butter

2 Tablespoons Whole Flaxseeds, Ground
1 Teaspoon Molasses

Preheat your oven to 375 degrees and line a baking sheet with a piece of parchment paper or a silpat.

Prepare the filling by first roughly mashing the banana in a large bowl. Mash in the applesauce, peanut butter, ground flaxseeds, and molasses, until well mixed and fairly smooth. A few chunks are just fine here. Set aside and let the filling sit for about 15 minutes to thicken.

Meanwhile, roll out your dough on a lightly floured surface into a rectangular shape, rather than the typical round for pie. Flatten the dough out to about ⅛ inch thick and cut out small rectangles approximately 2¼ x 3 inches.

When the filling is ready, spread about 2–4 teaspoons in the center of one small rectangle. Run lightly moistened fingers all the way around the edges to act as the "glue," and gently lay down a second dough rectangle on top. Use the tines of a fork to crimp and seal the edges together. Repeat with the remaining dough and filling, and transfer the tarts to your prepared sheet pan. Allow about ½ inch of space between them for the hot air to circulate evenly.

Bake for 12–16 minutes, until lightly golden brown all over. Let rest on the sheet pan for 5 minutes longer before transferring to a wire rack to finish cooling.

> These treats are much more perishable than the standard hard biscuits, so store them in the fridge for up to a week, or in the freezer for up to four months.

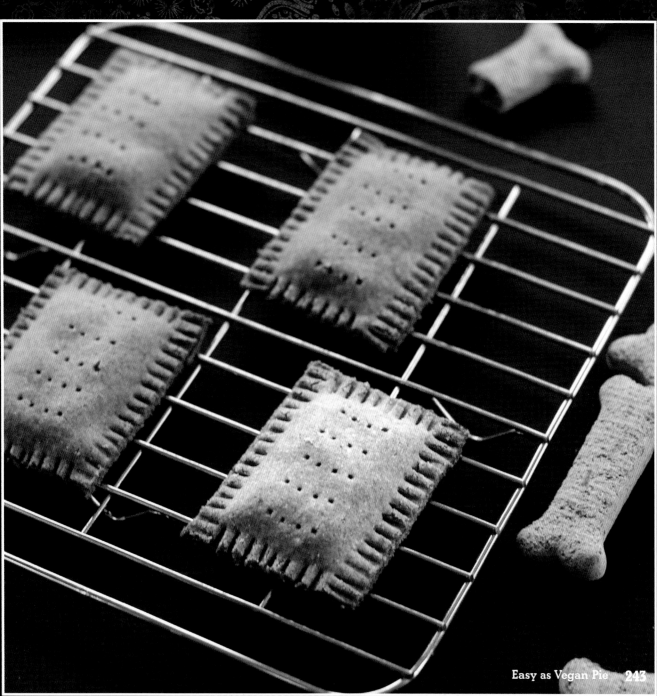

SNICKERDOODLE PIE

Makes 8–12 Servings

Acrisp, lightly caramelized topping of cinnamon sugar gives way to soft cookie dough, redolent of buttery vanilla. Easier than rolling out individual snickerdoodles and more gratifying than eating plain, cold cookie dough, there's no compromising with these rich slices. Though fantastic eaten at room temperature, it's even better when warmed and slightly gooey inside.

1 Unbaked Classic Crust (page 36) or
    Chocolate Pastry Crust (page 37)
Cookie Dough Filling:
2 Tablespoons Whole Flaxseeds
1 Cup All-Purpose Flour
½ Cup Granulated Sugar

¼ Cup Dark Brown Sugar, Firmly
    Packed
9 Tablespoons Non-Dairy Margarine
1 Tablespoon Vanilla Extract
½ Teaspoon Salt
¼ Teaspoon Baking Powder

¼ Teaspoon Ground Cinnamon
Cinnamon-Sugar Topping:
¼ Cup Turbinado Sugar
1½ Teaspoons Ground Cinnamon

Preheat your oven to 325 degrees.

For the filling, first grind the flaxseeds into a fine powder, and add it to a large bowl, along with the flour and both sugars. Melt the margarine and stir it into your dry ingredients. Follow with the vanilla, salt, baking powder, and cinnamon, stirring thoroughly to combine. This mixture will be very thick, similar to your standard cookie dough.

Press the dough-like filling evenly into your prepared crust, smoothing it out with a spatula. Mix together the turbinado sugar and cinnamon in a small bowl before sprinkling it evenly all over the top of the filling. Bake for 35 to 45 minutes, until the center appears to have puffed up a bit and the crust is golden brown. A toothpick inserted into the center should pull out cleanly. Let the pie cool for at least 20 minutes. If you let it cool all the way down to room temperature, reheat individual slices in the microwave to serve warm.

STAINED GLASS PIE

Makes 8–10 Servings

Jiggly, multi-colored cubes that bear no relationship to their fruity labels, gelatin snacks have never been my favorite. Even when my sister would beg for more, their strange, slippery charms were lost on me. If only I had discovered the joys of stained glass pie earlier! Beyond its aesthetic charm, one of the best aspects about this pie is how utterly versatile it is. Go for 100 percent fruit juice or fizzy sodas, and any flavor you fancy will work just as well. Pineapple juice is the only liquid that should be avoided, as it can't gel firmly when using agar.

1 Blind-Baked Chocolate Cookie Crust (page 48) or Vanilla Cookie Crust (page 48)

Stained Glass Cubes:

¾ Cup Strawberry Juice or Soda

¾ Cup Orange or Lemon Soda

¾ Cup Green Apple or Kiwi Soda

¾ Cup Blue Raspberry or Grape Soda

3 Teaspoons Agar Powder, Divided

Cream Gel:

1½ Cups Plain Non-Dairy Milk

⅔ Cup Granulated Sugar

2 Tablespoons Non-Dairy Margarine or Coconut Oil, Melted

1 Tablespoon Arrowroot Powder

1½ Teaspoons Agar Powder

⅛ Teaspoon Salt

1 Teaspoon Vanilla Extract

To make each of the colored cubes, the procedure is exactly the same. Lightly grease four mini loaf pans in preparation, and keep them nearby the stove. Vigorously whisk one of the juice or soda flavors at a time with ¾ teaspoon of agar, until the powder is fully dissolved. Heat in a small saucepan over medium-low heat, until the mixture comes to a rolling boil. Pour the hot liquid into one of the prepared loaf pans, rinse and thoroughly dry the saucepan, and repeat with the next flavor of juice or soda. When you have the agar cooked into all of the liquids separately, let the loaf pans sit at room temperature until completely cooled. Then, transfer to your fridge to finish solidifying, for at least 3–4 hours.

Once set, the rectangles of brightly colored agar should pop right out of the pans. Take one out at a time and slice it into even, ½-inch squares. Continue until all of your agar bricks are diced. Toss the various colors together and arrange them randomly in your prepared cookie crust. Don't pack them in too tightly; you want a bit of uneven overlap so that the cream gel can seep in between the cracks.

Combine the non-dairy milk, sugar, melted margarine or coconut oil, arrowroot, agar, and salt in a medium saucepan over moderate heat. Whisk vigorously to incorporate the starch and agar smoothly, with no lumps remaining. Cook until the mixture comes to a full boil before turning off the heat. Immediately pour into the pie shell, over and around the gelled cubes. It's perfectly fine if some of the cubes are still sticking out above the cream layer, as long as they're at least partially submerged so that they don't simply roll off the top later.

Allow the pie to rest at room temperature, undisturbed, until cooled to room temperature. Carefully move the whole thing into the fridge to chill and fully solidify. Let it rest for at least 3–4 hours before serving.

TORTA DI VERDURA

Makes 10–14 Servings

Is there no end to the kale craze? Will no one draw the line that not a leaf nor stem of kale shall cross? Clearly, that person isn't going to be me. The Italians have been throwing greens into desserts for centuries, long before it was avant-garde or the least bit trendy. Rather, it was thrifty, not to mention delicious above all else. A true torta di verdura is made with chard, but this blend of toothsome kale and more tender spinach better suits my tastes. Eat with an open mind and adventurous palate!

2 Unbaked Classic Crusts (page 36) or Wholesome Whole Wheat Crusts (page 44), 1 Unrolled

Verdura Filling:

2 Tablespoons Coconut Oil or Non-Dairy Margarine

1 Pound Fresh Curly Kale, Stems Removed and Torn into Bite-Sized Pieces

1 Pound Fresh Baby Spinach

¼ Cup Graham Cracker Crumbs (page 42)

½ Cup Plain Non-Dairy Milk

½ Cup Unsweetened Applesauce

½ Cup Light Agave Nectar

1 Cup Pitted Medjool Dates, Lightly Packed

½ Cup Toasted Pine Nuts or Sunflower Seeds

1 Teaspoon Ground Cinnamon

¼ Teaspoon Ground Nutmeg

¼ Teaspoon Ground Allspice

To Finish:

Golden Pastry Glaze (page 25)

Preheat your oven to 375 degrees.

You may think that this is a massive amount of greens in front of you, but don't worry, they cook down significantly in no time at all. Set a large stock pot over medium heat and begin by melting the coconut oil or margarine inside. Add the kale first, stirring to coat with the oil, and cook for 4–5 minutes until wilted. Toss in the spinach next and sauté for 2–3 minutes longer, until both greens are bright green, greatly reduced in volume, and tender. You should ultimately have 4 cups of cooked greens, lightly packed.

Let the greens cool to room temperature, then sprinkle in the graham cracker crumbs. Stir well before mixing in the applesauce and agave nectar next. Roughly mince the dates before tossing them into the mixture, along with the pine nuts and spices. Mix to distribute all of the ingredients evenly throughout.

Transfer the filling into the dough-lined pie pan, smoothing it out across the bottom. Roll out the upper crust to ⅛ inch thick and cut out long ½-inch wide strips. Lay on top in a lattice pattern (page 25) and lightly brush with golden pastry glaze.

Bake for 55–65 minutes until the pastry is golden brown. Let cool before serving. Slices taste great when accented with a dollop of whipped coconut cream (page 52) or vanilla ice cream (page 64).

SAVORY PIES

CARAMELIZED ONION AND APPLE TART

Makes 12–16 Servings

Brisk fall days bring more than just chilly temperatures and golden-hued leaves. Something in the air sounds the call for comfort food. Warming, simple meals will satisfy that craving, often incorporating any number of the freshly picked apple varieties now in markets. Tenderized after a long, slow simmer, their crispness fades but sweetness sings when paired with gently caramelized red onions. Though sweet in a very balanced way, the marriage is decidedly savory: an ideal side dish to a more meaty main, or a perfect appetizer for a party. Just the smell of the apples, onions, and herbs cooking away in the kitchen can soothe the soul, welcoming the autumn season in the most delicious way.

1 Sheet Frozen Puff Pastry, Thawed
Caramelized Apples and Onions:
3 Tablespoons Olive Oil
2 Pounds (About 3–4 Medium) Red Onions, Halved and Thinly Sliced
¾–1 Teaspoon Salt

1 Large Sweet Apple (Such as Fuji, Braeburn, or Golden Delicious), Peeled, Cored, and Sliced
1 Large Tart Apple (Such as Granny Smith or Mutsu), Peeled, Cored, and Sliced
½ Teaspoon Dried Thyme

¼ Teaspoon Ground Black Pepper
2 Tablespoons Dry White Wine
2 Tablespoons Balsamic Vinegar
To Finish:
½ Cup Raw Walnuts, Roughly Chopped
Fresh Thyme (Optional, for Garnish)

Preheat your oven to 400 degrees and line a baking sheet with parchment paper or a silpat.

Pour the oil into a medium skillet over moderate heat, adding in the onion when hot. Cook, stirring frequently, for about 15 minutes, or until lightly golden brown all over. You don't want to simply brown the edges here, but cook the onion evenly all over, which is why the pan can't be left unattended. Add ¼ teaspoon of the salt, which will draw out more moisture and help prevent the onion from sticking or burning.

Toss in the apple slices next, along with the thyme, pepper, wine, and vinegar. Stir well to incorporate, and turn the heat down to medium-low. Let simmer for about 15–20 minutes longer, until the apples are fork-tender and there is no remaining excess liquid in the pan. Turn off the stove and let cool for at least 15 minutes.

Meanwhile, roll out the puff pastry on a lightly floured surface to about ⅛ inch thick, and cut it into two equally-sized, long, skinny rectangles. Place them both on your prepared baking sheet, with at least an inch of space in between them.

Distribute the filling equally over the pastry, leaving a ½ inch border of dough clear around the edges. Sprinkle chopped walnuts over the top, and bake for 15–20 minutes, until the pastry has puffed around the filling and turned golden brown. Let cool for at least 10 minutes before slicing and serving. Sprinkle a pinch of fresh thyme over the warm tarts if desired and serve warm.

CHEESY MAC PIE

Makes 10–14
Servings

Whether it was lovingly made from scratch by mom or came straight out of the blue box, macaroni and cheese has been a staple comfort food for even the pickiest eaters. Something about those toothsome noodles and mild, salty cheese sauce beg for just one more bite, until the whole bowlful has disappeared. Although stovetop was the only way to go when I was younger, I've since discovered the joys of a good bread crumb topping, adding complexity in both crunchy texture and a darker, toasted flavor. Supporting that fool-proof combination with a sturdy crust seems like a natural next step, since baked mac is already transferred into the oven for a second kiss of heat. Throw in a token green vegetable like broccoli, and all of a sudden the classic mac is all grown up, complete with all the original comfort but none of the guilt.

1 Unbaked Classic Crust (page 36), Wholesome Whole Wheat Crust (page 44), or Cornmeal Crust (page 38)

Cheesy Sauce:
1 Cup Peeled and Diced Yukon Gold Potatoes (1 Medium, 8-Ounce Potato)
½ Cup Diced Carrot (1 Medium, 3-Ounce Carrot)
⅔ Cup Chopped Yellow Onion (½ Medium, 4.5-Ounce Onion)
1 Clove Garlic, Thinly Sliced
1¼ Cups Water

½ Cup Raw Cashews
¼ Cup Nutritional Yeast
2 Tablespoons All-Purpose Flour
2 Tablespoons Brown Rice Miso Paste
1 Tablespoon Tomato Paste
½ Teaspoon Dijon Mustard
2 Teaspoons Rice Vinegar
½ Teaspoon Smoked Paprika
⅛ Teaspoon Turmeric (Optional, for Color)
1¼ Cups Unsweetened Non-Dairy Milk
⅓ Cup Canola Oil or Any Neutral Vegetable Oil

¼–½ Teaspoon Salt
Filling:
1 Pound Small Elbow Pasta, Undercooked by 2–3 Minutes and Thoroughly Drained
1 Head Broccoli, Chopped into Bite-Sized Florets (About 2 Cups Florets) and Lightly Steamed

Bread Crumb Topping:
1 Cup Panko Bread Crumbs
⅛ Teaspoon Smoked Paprika
1 Tablespoon Canola Oil

Place the cut potatoes, carrots, onion, and garlic in a small saucepan, and pour in the water. Set over medium heat on the stove, and bring to a boil. Once the water reaches a vigorous boil, cover the pot, turn down the heat to medium-low, and let simmer for 15 minutes, until the potatoes are extremely tender.

Continued on page 256.

Meanwhile, prep the other ingredients to speed things along. Place the cashews, nutritional yeast, salt, mustard, lemon juice, paprika, and turmeric (if using) in your blender. A high-speed blender is recommended for the best results, but you can also use an ordinary machine as long as you have patience. Give these ingredients a light pulse to begin breaking down the cashews.

When the vegetables on the stove are fully cooked and ready, pour them into your blender along with all of the cooking water. Add in ¾ cup of the non-dairy milk, and turn on the blender to its highest setting. Thoroughly puree the mixture, until completely smooth and lump-free. If you're using a less powerful blender, this could take 6–10 minutes. With the motor still running, slowly drizzle in the oil, to allow it to properly emulsify. Check the consistency; if you like your sauce a bit thinner, blend in the remaining ¼ of non-dairy milk.

Pour the sauce over your cooked noodles and broccoli, tossing to thoroughly coat. Transfer to your waiting unbaked crust.

For the topping, simply stir together all of the ingredients before sprinkling evenly over the cheesy macaroni. Bake in 350 degree oven for 35–45 minutes, until the breadcrumbs are golden brown. Let cool for at least 5 minutes before serving. For more cohesive slices, allow the pie to fully cool before cutting.

FRIED GREEN TOMATO PIES

Makes 12–14 Servings

Hanging stubbornly onto their vines late into the final days of summer, still hard as green stones, unripe tomatoes are the bane of many a gardener's existence. Punishingly sour, you'd never want to eat one out of hand. . . . But something magical happens when it hits the scalding oil of the deep fryer. Mellowed by the richness of the oil and coated in a shatteringly crisp batter, those ugly late bloomers can still get all the glory they deserve.

1 Unbaked and Unrolled Classic
   Crust (page 36) or Cornmeal
   Crust (page 38)
Green Tomato Filling:
2 Medium Green Tomatoes (About 1
   Cup Chopped)
2 Tablespoons All-Purpose Flour
2 Tablespoons Coarse Yellow
   Cornmeal

½ Teaspoon Salt
1 Teaspoon Smoked Paprika
¼ Teaspoon Dried Oregano
¼ Teaspoon Dried Basil
¼ Teaspoon Ground Black Pepper
¼ Teaspoon Cayenne Pepper
Avocado Aioli:
¼ Cup Raw Cashews, Soaked for 2–4
   Hours

3 Cloves Garlic
1 Medium Ripe Avocado
2 Tablespoons Lemon Juice
½ Teaspoon Lemon Zest
¼ Teaspoon Salt
¼–⅓ Cup Water
To Finish:
Oil for Frying

The aioli can be made 4–5 days in advance, so to streamline the cooking process, go ahead and prepare that first. Thoroughly rinse and drain the cashews before tossing them into your blender or food processor, along with the remaining ingredients for the aioli. Puree, pausing periodically to scrape down the sides of the bowl to make sure there are no lumps remaining. Once smooth, transfer aioli to an airtight container. Place a piece of plastic wrap directly on the surface of the dip before sealing the container and storing it in the fridge.

Moving on to the pies, chop the green tomatoes into raisin-sized pieces and toss them in a large bowl with the flour, cornmeal, salt, herbs, and spices. Stir well so that the tomato pieces are all evenly coated with the dry goods.

Meanwhile, pour enough oil into a high-sided skillet or deep stock pot to reach a depth of ¾ inch, and turn on stove to high. Use a deep-frying or candy thermometer to know when the oil hits 375 degrees.

For the crusts, roll out your prepared and chilled crust on a lightly floured surface. Aim for an even ⅛ inch thickness all around. Using round cookie cutters about 4 inches in diameter, cut out as many circles of dough as your crust will allow. Gather any scraps, re-roll, and repeat as needed, until the dough is used up.

Continued on page 259.

Spoon about 1 heaping tablespoon of tomato filling into the center of each circle. It may not seem like a lot, but a little filling does go a long way. Using lightly moistened fingers, trace the inner rim of the circles to act as "glue", fold them in half and press down gently but firmly around the half-moons. Use a fork dipped in flour to go back over the edge and crimp the pies. Finally, poke the fork into the top of each pie once, to create steam vents.

Carefully ease 2 or 3 pies at a time into the hot oil, to prevent the pan from becoming too crowded. Cook for 3–5 minutes per side, flipping gently with a slotted spatula or wire spider. Transfer to an overturned cooling rack set on paper towels, and let cool for at least 10 minutes before enjoying so that you don't burn your mouth! Repeat the frying process for the remaining pies.

Serve with a generous dollop of avocado aioli on the side.

PRIMAVERA POT PIES

**Makes 2–4
Servings**

Cradled in a flaky, golden crust, asparagus and fava beans commingle with the standard mirepoix, mushrooms, and savory spices. Just creamy enough without being overly rich or heavy, this is one hearty spring meal that won't weigh you down. Topped off with tender potatoes, crisped around the edges and finished with coarse sea salt, it's one stunning entree to present to a loved one. And let me tell you, you had better REALLY love that special someone, because this is admittedly a good deal of work for two servings. If you don't have a huge appetite, it could be stretched to perhaps 3 or 4. . . . But based on the delectable taste, I can make no guarantees. Save this one for a special occasion—you're sure to win some serious brownie points!

1 Unbaked and Unrolled Classic
   Crust (page 36) or Wholesome
   Whole Wheat Crust (page 44)
Stewed Primavera Filling:
2 Tablespoons Olive Oil
1 Medium Carrot, Peeled and Finely
   Diced
1 Stalk Celery, Diced
½ Small Yellow Onion, Diced
1 Skinny Leek, Quartered
   Lengthwise, Rinsed Thoroughly,
   and Chopped

1 Cup Roughly Chopped Crimini or
   Button Mushrooms
½ Teaspoon Salt
1 Teaspoon Cornstarch
½ Cup Unsweetened Non-Dairy Milk
2 Tablespoons Dry White Wine
1 Teaspoon Red Wine Vinegar
1 Bay Leaf
2 Teaspoons Nutritional Yeast
¼ Teaspoon Poultry Seasoning
¼ Teaspoon Hot Paprika
Pinch Freshly Ground Black Pepper

1½ Cups Shelled and Skinned
   Fresh Fava Beans, or Frozen and
   Defrosted
1 Cup Chopped Asparagus (½-Inch
   Pieces)
¼ Cup Fresh Parsley, Roughly
   Chopped
Potato Top Crust:
1 Medium (8-Ounce) Russet Potato
1½ Teaspoons Olive Oil
Pinch Coarse Sea Salt
To Finish:
Fresh Chopped Chives or Scallion

Chill your dough, then turn it out on a lightly floured surface and roll it out gently, as thinly as possible without creating holes. Approximately ⅛ inch is ideal. Lightly oil two glass or ceramic dishes that can hold about 2–3 cups each, and cut out rounds of pastry slightly larger than the bowls. Ease the pastry into each prepared dish, and use your fingers to smooth out the corners and sides. Press the pastry hard against the rim of the dishes to trim it, and leave a tiny bit of

Preheat your oven to 375 degrees, and set to work on the filling next.

Place a large pot or sauté pan over medium heat, and add in the oil. Once hot, toss in the prepared carrots, celery, onions, leeks, and mushrooms, and cook, stirring occasionally, for about 10 minutes. Once softened and lightly browned, add in the salt and cornstarch, stirring well to thoroughly coat the vegetables in the starch. Pour in the "milk," wine, and vinegar, and mix vigorously to prevent lumps from forming. Next, incorporate the bay leaf, nutritional yeast, poultry seasoning, paprika, and black pepper to taste. Turn down the heat to medium-low and simmer for about 15 minutes.

Meanwhile, pull out your mandoline if you've got one, and slice the potato into coins about 1 mm thick. You can also do this by hand with a sharp knife, patience, and precision. Toss the slices with oil and set aside.

Turn off the heat on the filling, and toss in the fava beans, asparagus, and parsley at the last possible moment—you don't want them to get over-cooked in the oven. Mix well to distribute the veggies. Divide the filling evenly between your two pastry-lined dishes, and place both on a baking sheet for easier removal from the oven, and to catch any accidental drips. Layer your potatoes in a circular pattern on top of each pie, and finish each with a light sprinkle of coarse salt. You will likely have extra potato coins, but hang on to them; they make fantastic chips. Move the assembled pies into the preheated oven, and bake for 45–50 minutes, until the crust is lightly golden brown and the potatoes are browned around the edges. In case the potatoes threaten to burn, tent the pies with aluminum foil about 35 minutes into the baking process.

Let cool for at least 10–15 minutes before serving, and finish with a sprinkle of chopped chives or scallion, if desired.

REUBEN PIE

Makes 8–10
Servings

Some say it's the king of sandwiches, and by the way some traditional delis pile the fillings sky-high, it sure does have looks that fit the title. Hot corned beef is smothered with thousand island dressing, sauerkraut, and cheese, served up piping hot between two slices of rye bread. I remember watching in awe as a sandwich big enough to feed a small family was delivered to my dad on one fateful day at the deli counter, but even as a child I felt no compulsion to give it a taste. The allure of the Great Reuben never quite caught on with me, until I discovered that it was making waves even in the vegan culinary scene. I'll level with all the serious meat eaters out there and say outright that my corned seitan will never taste exactly the same. No sir . . . It's so much better. Beef only wishes it were so lean and flavorful all at once.

Don't be scared off by the lengthy recipe and list of ingredients. It simply takes a number of different components, each of which comes together quickly and can be prepared in advance. To cut down on some of the work, feel free to use your favorite ready-made thousand island or Russian dressing.

Corned Seitan:

2 Cups Water

1 Small (2-Ounce) Red Beet, Cooked, Peeled, and Sliced*

¼ Cup Reduced Sodium Soy Sauce

1 Tablespoon Dark Brown Sugar, Firmly Packed

1 Clove Garlic, Finely Minced

1 Teaspoon Onion Powder

1 Teaspoon Whole Black Mustard Seeds

¾ Teaspoon Whole Celery Seeds

½ Teaspoon Ground Coriander

¼ Teaspoon Ground Black Pepper

¼ Teaspoon Ground Ginger

⅛ Teaspoon Ground Cloves

⅛ Teaspoon Ground Allspice

⅛ Teaspoon Ground Cinnamon

2 Bay Leaves

1 Pound Cooked Seitan, Cut into ⅛-Inch Thick Slices

To Finish:

2 Unbaked Rye Crusts (page 45), 1 Unrolled

2 Tablespoons Dijon Mustard

½ Cup Thousand Island Dressing (page 265)

1¼ Cups Sauerkraut, Thoroughly Drained

1–2 Tablespoons Plain Non-Dairy Milk

*See page 110 for beet cooking tips.

To make the corned seitan, simply toss all of the ingredients into a medium saucepan and bring to a rolling boil. Cover the pan, turn off the heat, and let marinate at room temperature for at least 8 hours. Move the whole mixture into

Continued on page 265.

the fridge if you'd like to let it marinate overnight, but no more than 16 hours. The seitan will have developed a light pink tint due to the beet, and should be sweet, spicy, and subtly salty when it's done. Drain the seitan thoroughly and remove the whole spices. You can either discard the excess marinade or reserve it to make a second batch of seitan, or get creative in making various pickled vegetables.

Preheat your oven to 375 degrees.

Smear the mustard across the bottom crust-lined pie pan dough before piling the corned seitan on top, overlapping pieces lengthwise to allow for the most tightly packed, even layer possible. Drizzle the dressing all over, and finish with a covering of kraut. Roll out the second rye crust and cut into strips to make a lattice top if desired, or make a plain, vented upper crust. Brush the top crust all over with the non-dairy milk of your choosing.

Bake 35–40 minutes or until the crust is golden brown. Let cool for at least 15 minutes before slicing and chowing down.

Thousand Island Dressing:

1 12-Ounce Aseptic Package Extra-Firm Silken Tofu
½ Cup Tomato Paste
⅓ Cup Olive Oil

2 Tablespoons Apple Cider Vinegar
1 Tablespoon Braggs Liquid Aminos or Reduced-Sodium Soy Sauce
2 Teaspoons Amber Agave Nectar
1½ Teaspoons Onion Powder

¼ Teaspoon Freshly Ground Black Pepper
⅓–½ Cup Finely Chopped Dill Pickles

Toss everything except for the pickles into either your blender or food processor, and thoroughly puree. Pause to scrape down the sides of the bowl periodically, ensuring that there are no chunks of tofu left behind. Once silky-smooth, stir in the chopped pickles by hand, and enjoy on sandwiches, salads, and for dipping raw vegetables.

Reuben Deluxe Pie: Add 1 cup shredded mozzarella-style vegan cheese and ½ cup coconut bacon (page 51).

SPAGHETTI SQUASH AND MEATBALL PIE

Makes 8-10 Servings

Ever snap up one of those oblong, yellow spaghetti squash at the arrival of fall and then find yourself flummoxed when it comes time to cook it? Not to worry, there's a reason why we tend to collect them as accidental kitchen decorations each year. Instead, put them to good use and make them into something way better than plain stringy squash! Though the "crust" created here isn't crisp like traditional pastry, it's the perfect edible vessel for a hearty serving of "sauce and balls." Every bit as satisfying as noodles but without the carb coma after eating, spaghetti squash is a fun way to sneak in an extra serving of vegetables without even realizing it. If the clock is ticking and dinner should have been on the table an hour ago, this dish can also be completed without being baked into a pie shape; it's okay, I won't tell the pie police. Just toss the cooked squash noodles with sauce and add in as many meatless balls as your heart (and stomach) desires.

Spaghetti Squash Crust:
1 3-Pound Spaghetti Squash
½ Cup Water
1 Tablespoon Whole Flaxseeds
1 Tablespoon Chia Seeds
1 Tablespoon Cornstarch
2 Tablespoons Nutritional Yeast
½ Teaspoon Italian Seasoning*
¼ Teaspoon Salt
⅔ Cup Water
2 Tablespoons Non-Dairy Margarine
   or Coconut Oil, Melted

Meatless Balls:
2 Tablespoons Olive Oil, Divided
½ Medium Yellow Onion, Diced
2 Cloves Garlic, Finely Minced
1 Cup Raw Sunflower Seeds
¾ Cup Cooked Brown or Green
   Lentils**
2 Tablespoons Soy Sauce
2 Teaspoons Dried Parsley
1 Teaspoon Dried Basil
½ Teaspoon Dried Oregano
¼ Teaspoon Smoked Paprika

¼ Teaspoon Crushed Red Pepper
   Flakes
1 Tablespoon Whole Flaxseeds,
   Ground

To Finish:
1¼ Cups Prepared Marinara or
   Spaghetti Sauce
2–3 Tablespoons Pepita Parm (page
   62) or Shredded Vegan Cheese,
   Optional

The meatless balls will be the most time-consuming part of this pie, but you can prepare them up to a week in advance and store in an airtight container in the fridge.

Heat 1 tablespoon of the oil over medium heat and add in the onions and garlic. Sauté gently until aromatic and lightly browned, about 10 minutes. Add in the sunflower seeds and let toast lightly for 2–3 minutes. Move everything into the bowl of your food processor, and grind it down to a coarse meal. Introduce all of the remaining ingredients for the balls next, and pulse until well-combined and cohesive. You don't want it pureed, but with a bit of texture remaining. Refrigerate the mixture until thoroughly chilled, approximately 2 hours. This will make it much easier to handle.

Continued on page 268.

Scoop the meatless mix with a small cookie scoop or two spoons and roll into approximately walnut-sized balls. Keep them a bit smaller than you would for normal meatballs so that you can fit more into a single slice. You should end up with 20–24 balls; this will likely result in some leftover after completing the pie.

Clean out the sauté pan and heat the remaining tablespoon of oil over medium heat. When hot, place about half of the balls into the pan and lightly fry for about 10 minutes, rolling gently with a spatula to brown all sides. Transfer the cooked balls onto a plate and repeat with the remaining half. Set aside.

Preheat your oven to 350 degrees and lightly grease a 10-inch round pie pan.

Cut the squash in half lengthwise, removing the inner membrane and seeds with a large spoon. Either discard or save the seeds to bake later as crunchy snacks.*** Place both halves, cut sides up, in a microwave-safe dish and fill each cavity with ¼ cup water. Cover with a piece of microwavable plastic wrap. Microwave for 10 minutes and let it sit for 5 minutes longer. Once cool enough to handle, use a fork to scrape noodle-like strands into a large bowl.

To create the "glue" that will both bind and flavor the crust, begin by grinding both seeds down to a fine powder and mix with cornstarch, nutritional yeast, Italian seasoning, salt, and water; let stand for at least 5 minutes to thicken. Pour the mixture over your cooked spaghetti squash, followed immediately by the melted margarine or coconut oil. Toss to coat.

Transfer the squash into your prepared pie pan, easing it up the sides so that it evenly covers the whole surface. Add half of the sauce into the bottom, distributing half of the balls on top. Redistribute as needed to form a fairly even layer before following with the remaining sauce and balls. Finish with an even sprinkle of pepita parm or vegan cheese of your choosing, if desired.

Bake for 30–35 minutes or until heated through and the edges of the squash are lightly browned.

*Consider this a guideline more than a rule, but for a traditional Italian seasoning, you can't go wrong with 3 tablespoons each dried basil, dried oregano, and dried parsley, 1 tablespoon garlic powder, 1 teaspoon dried thyme, ½ teaspoon dried, powdered rosemary, and ¼ teaspoon ground black pepper.

**The best method that I've encountered for cooking tender yet toothsome lentils is to treat them like pasta. For every cup of dry lentils, bring a quart of water to a boil before tossing the legumes in. Nudge the heat down slightly to a lively simmer and cook for 20–25 minutes, until tender. Drain thoroughly and use as desired. Note that this will not work for red lentils, which can only be cooked to a fairly soupy consistency.

***Waste not, want not! The seeds of any squash can be tossed with a splash of olive oil and a sprinkle of salt before baking to a crunchy finish, just like pumpkin seeds. Bake them at 300 degrees for about 45 minutes, stirring occasionally, until evenly browned all over. Let cool completely before snacking or storing in an airtight container at room temperature.

TACO PIE

Makes 6–8 servings

It may not be a traditional taco, but this family-style rendition bears the very same heart and soul. Piquant tempeh cradled in a buttery cornmeal crust is just the beginning; the sky is the limit for toppings, and the more the merrier. Season your pie just the way you like your tacos, and you've got yourself an instant fiesta for any dinner.

1 Unbaked Cornmeal Crust (page 38) in a 9-Inch Deep-Dish Pie Pan

Tempeh Taco Meat:
2 8-Ounce Packages Tempeh
2 Tablespoons Olive Oil
1 Small or ½ Large Red Onion, Diced
2 Cloves Garlic, Finely Minced
6 Ounces Cremini or Button Mushrooms, Roughly Minced (About 2 Cups)
1 Cup Vegetable Stock or Water
1¼ Cups Prepared Salsa*

1 14-Ounce Can (1¾ Cup) Cooked Black Beans, Rinsed and Drained
2 Tablespoons Soy Sauce
1 Tablespoon Chili Powder
1½ Teaspoons Ground Cumin
1¼ Teaspoons Smoked Paprika
¼ Teaspoon Crushed Red Pepper Flakes
¼ Teaspoon Cayenne Pepper
½ Teaspoon Dried Oregano
½–1 Teaspoon Salt
¼ Cup All-Purpose Flour

Sour Cream Topping:
1 Cup Vegan Sour Cream
1 Tablespoon Lime Juice

To Finish:
1 Heart Romaine Lettuce, Chopped
½ Red Bell Pepper, Finely Diced

Optional Topping Ideas:
Sliced Black Olives, Fresh Cilantro or Parsley, Shredded Vegan Cheese, Diced Avocado, Pickled Jalapenos, or Additional Salsa.

Preheat your oven to 375 degrees and line a 9-inch deep-dish pie pan with your prepared and rolled-out crust. Place it in the fridge while you attend to the filling.

Chop the tempeh into small squares and place them in a medium saucepan with water to cover. Bring to a boil, then reduce the heat slightly and simmer gently. This will help remove some of the bitterness, and also tenderize the tempeh. After 15 minutes, drain thoroughly and set aside.

In a large saucepan or stock pot, heat the oil over moderate heat, and toss in the diced onion. After about 5 minutes, when the onion is softened and aromatic, add in the garlic and mushrooms. Stir periodically as the veggies cook, to prevent them from burning. When the liquid released by the mushrooms has evaporated and the vegetables begin to stick to the pan, quickly deglaze with the stock and salsa.

Continued on page 271.

Finally, incorporate the prepared tempeh, black beans, tamari, and all of the spices. Reduce the heat just a touch and simmer for 10–15 minutes, until the flavors meld and the liquid has been mostly absorbed. Add salt to taste, and then let the mixture stand off the heat for 15 minutes, to cool slightly. Very slowly sprinkle the flour over the surface in four separate additions, stirring each addition in completely before moving on to the next, to prevent clumping.

Retrieve your chilled crust from the fridge and pile in the tempeh filling. Smooth out the top with a spatula, and slide the pan into the oven. Bake 20 minutes. Meanwhile, mix together the "sour cream" and lime juice, and pour this topping over the pie after the initial baking period. Smooth it out evenly, and return the pie to the oven for a final 10–15 more minutes, until the top appears dry. Don't worry if the smooth white layer cracks while baking or after cooling, since you'll cover up any blemishes with a bright handful of greens later.

Carefully remove the pie from the oven, and let cool for at least 15 minutes before topping with lettuce, peppers, and any other additional toppings your heart desires. Slice and serve for dinner!

*Now *is* the time to play favorites! Pick a salsa you already enjoy eating, and you'll like the pie a whole lot more. Any salsa goes, be it mild or three-alarm spicy, red or green, so just use what you have and season according to taste.

TAMALE PIES

Taking the initial plunge into veganism at a young age, I had yet to develop any culinary skills when I suddenly found myself alone in the kitchen. Though supportive, my parents made it clear that I was to cook my own meals from that point forward, being the only vegan (or even vegetarian) in the family. More often than not, that meant a tofu pup skewered and "grilled" over an open stovetop burner, or terribly waxy slices of "cheese" warmed between two slices of rubbery whole wheat bread. It was not an auspicious start to a successful career in food, and I would have likely starved in those early years if not for a few merciful frozen meals. Tamale pies, individual cardboard bowls filled with mildly spiced beans and vegetables, topped off with a thin sheet of soft polenta, were my saving grace in high school. Something about their comforting simplicity quickly elevated those miniature pies to the top of my dinner list, even though they could be painfully difficult to find. If only I had thought to try making them at home sooner! Though I try to stay fairly true to my fond memories, these particular pies do have a bit more heat, but are of course adjustable for more sensitive palates.

Bean and Vegetable Tamale Filling:
2 Tablespoons Olive oil
½ Cup Diced Yellow Onion
1 Clove Garlic, Finely Minced
1¼ Cups Diced Zucchini
½ Cup Chopped Red Bell Pepper
½–1 Jalapeño Pepper, Finely Minced
1 Teaspoon Ground Cumin

½ Teaspoon Chili Powder
½ Teaspoon Salt
½ Teaspoon Dried Oregano
¼ Teaspoon Dried Basil
1 Cup Cooked Pinto Beans
1 Cup Cooked Black Beans
1 Cup Corn Kernels, Fresh or Frozen
   and Thawed

1 14.5-Ounce Can Fire-Roasted,
   Diced Tomatoes, Drained
¼ Cup Tomato Paste
Polenta Topping:
2 Cups Vegetable Broth, Divided
½ Cup Coarse Yellow Corn Meal
⅛ Teaspoon Salt
⅛ Teaspoon Ground Black Pepper

Preheat your oven to 350 degrees and lightly grease six 4-ounce ramekins.

Set a medium-size skillet over moderate heat and add in the oil. Once hot, toss in the onion and cook for about 2–3 minutes, until translucent. Add the garlic next, sautéing the two together for another 6–8 minutes, at which point they should be aromatic and golden around the edges. Next, add the zucchini and both peppers, stirring gently and cooking 5–8 more minutes, until the vegetables all begin to brown lightly. Stir in the all of the spices, herbs, and salt, cooking for just a minute longer to release the essential oils.

Stir in the beans, corn, tomatoes, and tomato paste, taking care to work out any lumps of tomato paste before proceeding. Let the whole stew simmer gently for 5 minutes to meld the flavors before taking the pan off the heat. Spoon the filling into your prepared ramekins, doling out equal amounts to all six.

Get started on the topping by bringing 1½ cups of the broth to a boil in a medium saucepan. In a separate bowl, whisk together the cornmeal, the remaining stock, salt, and pepper. Once smooth, slowly pour it into the saucepan full of hot stock while whisking constantly but gently, taking care not to splash. As it gets thicker, continue to scrape the bottom and sides of the saucepan as you stir, to prevent anything from sticking and burning. Bubbles will break rapidly on the surface, at which point you'll know it's done. Make haste and pour the hot polenta over the tops of the filled ramekins, since it will solidify as it cools.

Use a spatula to further smooth the topping out over the filling, spreading it all the way to the edges to fully cover the stew. Place the ramekins on a large baking sheet for easy maneuvering in and out of the oven, giving them a good bit of breathing space between them so that the hot air can circulate. Bake for 30–35 minutes, until cornmeal topping has firmed up and the filling is bubbling up around edges. Let cool for at least 10 minutes before eating.

TEA TART

Afternoon tea time is a treasured British ritual that sadly has yet to catch on in the states. Not only does it place a restorative breather in the middle of a hard day's work, but it comes complete with snacks to stave off hunger until dinner arrives. Cucumber sandwiches are the quintessential nibble, as dainty as they are simple. Fluffy white bread contains a tangy smear of cream cheese, lightened with thinly sliced cucumbers; nothing more, nothing less. Of course, it's hard to leave well enough alone, and it turns out there is room for improvement, even in something so close to perfection. Fresh herbs and the peppery bite of crisp radishes invigorate this classic combination. Consider this tart transformation merely an open-faced sandwich meant for sharing.

1 Blind-Baked Classic Crust (page 36)
1 8-Ounce Container Vegan Cream Cheese
½ Teaspoon Lemon Zest

2 Tablespoons Fresh Parsley, Roughly Chopped
¼ Cup Fresh Dill, Roughly Chopped
3–4 Tablespoons Fresh Chives, Thinly Sliced

Salt and Ground Black Pepper, to Taste
2–3 Persian Cucumbers or ½ Large Seedless Cucumber, Thinly Sliced
4–5 Radishes, Thinly Sliced

After the crust is baked, this tart needs no additional heat, so you can go ahead and turn off the oven.

In a medium bowl, beat together the cream cheese, lemon zest, parsley, dill, and chives, until creamy and flecked with herbs throughout. Add salt and pepper to taste, and mix once more. Transfer the spread to your cooked and cooled crust, smoothing it evenly into the bottom. Arrange the slices of cucumber and radishes overlapping in concentric circles on top, alternating the two vegetables, until the cream cheese layer is covered. Chill for at least an hour before serving.

THANKSGIVING QUICHE

Serves 12–14

The day after Thanksgiving, or perhaps the day after that if you're the type with family that likes to stick around, once the dust has settled, it's time to use or lose those valuable leftovers. Easier is better after slaving over the original meal in the first place, so an all-inclusive meal like quiche sounded too appealing for me to resist. The beauty of this is that absolutely anything can be tucked away into that "eggy" chickpea mixture, so no matter what you still have on hand, it can find a welcoming home here. Just don't try to hide any marshmallow-topped potato abomination within the depths of an honest savory quiche; it's a gross misuse of vegan marshmallows from the start, and just plain wrong. Not that I have strong opinions about such things . . .

1 Unbaked Classic Crust (page 36), Cornmeal Crust (page 38), or Wholesome Whole Wheat Crust (page 44), 1 Unrolled

1 Cup Vegan "Turkey," Seitan, or Tempeh, Diced or Shredded

½ Cup Green Beans or Brussels Sprouts, Chopped into Bite-Sized Pieces

1 Cup Roasted Butternut Squash, Pumpkin, or Potatoes, Cubed

½ Cup Roughly Chopped Cremini or Button Mushrooms

1 Stalk Celery, Finely Diced

½ Small Leek, Cleaned, Greens Removed, and Thinly Sliced

3–5 Cloves Garlic, Minced

1 Cup Garbanzo Bean Flour

2 Tablespoons Potato Starch or Cornstarch

4 Teaspoons Nutritional Yeast

½ Teaspoon Dried Thyme

¼ Teaspoon Dried Ground Sage

¼ Teaspoon Sweet Paprika

¼ Teaspoon Ground Cumin

¼ Teaspoon Baking Powder

1 Cup Vegetable Stock or Water

¾ Cup Unsweetened Non-Dairy Milk

½ Cup Pumpkin Puree

2 Tablespoons Olive Oil

1 Tablespoon Soy Sauce

2 Teaspoons Dijon Mustard

¼ Cup Raw Pepitas (Optional)

Preheat your oven to 350 degrees and have your pie crust at the ready.

Prepare your protein and veggies as indicated in the ingredient list, straight through to the garlic, and mix them all together in a large bowl. Set aside.

In a separate bowl, whisk together the chickpea/garbanzo flour, potato starch, nutritional yeast, salt, herbs, spices, and baking powder. Pour in the vegetable stock or water, non-dairy milk, pumpkin puree, oil, soy sauce, and mustard, and whisk until smooth. It should be about the consistency of pancake batter. Pour this batter into your bowl of prepared veggies, and stir gently to combine but not smash any of the ingredients. Transfer the whole mixture into your waiting pie crust, and if there's extra, pour it into lightly greased 4-ounce ramekins. Lightly tap the pan(s) on the counter a few times to release any air bubbles. Place quiche and ramekins, if using, on a baking sheet to make them easier to transport into and out of the oven. Sprinkle the top(s) with pepitas, if desired.

Bake the quiche for 45–55 minutes, until the filling appears set and it's lightly golden brown on top. Keep a close eye on the little ramekins, and expect them to be done in closer to 30 minutes; be prepared to pull them out so that they don't over-bake. Let cool for at least 15 minutes before slicing. (The leftovers also taste great cold, in my opinion!)

Serve with cranberry sauce or gravy, if desired.

WASABI PEA PIE

Serves 8–10

Wasabi peas are HOT, and not just in flavor! What were once strange, obscure imports have now proliferated and spread the furthest corners of globe. They can even be found in many gas stations among the other snacks, if that says anything about their widespread appeal. It's not hard to understand the attraction; their characteristic crunch and satisfying afterburn explain everything. Why not manipulate those very same winning qualities to make something decidedly more savory, not to mention worthy of a meal? Green pea flour can be somewhat difficult to find in mainstream markets, so standard chickpea flour is a fine substitution, and doesn't stray too far from the title either.

1 Unbaked Classic Crust (page 36)
Wasabi-Pea Filling:
1¼ Cups Green Pea Flour
1½–2 Tablespoons Wasabi Powder,
    or 1–1½ Tablespoons Wasabi
    Paste

¾ Teaspoon Salt
⅛ Teaspoon Ground Black Pepper
2 Cups Frozen Green Peas, Thawed
2–3 Scallions, Thinly Sliced
1 Tablespoon White Miso Paste
1 Teaspoon Prepared Horseradish

2 Cups Vegetable or Mushroom Broth
3 Tablespoons Rice Vinegar
¼ Cup Olive Oil
To Finish:
½ Cup Crushed Wasabi Peas

Preheat your oven to 350 degrees.

Whisk together the green pea flour, powdered wasabi, salt, and black pepper. Add in the peas and scallions, tossing to coat. In a separate bowl, whisk the miso paste and horseradish into your vegetable or mushroom broth, stirring until dissolved. Pour the stock, vinegar, and oil into the bowl of dry goods all at the same time, and whisk until smooth (aside from the peas and scallions, of course). Pour this batter into your waiting crust and lightly tap the pan on the counter a few times to release any air bubbles. Sprinkle the crushed wasabi peas evenly over the entire exposed surface.

Bake for 40–50 minutes, until the filling appears set and ever so lightly golden brown on top. Let cool for at least 15 minutes before slicing. Serve hot or at room temperature.

INDEX